OUT OF OLD
NOVA SCOTIA
KITCHENS

To my husband and sons
and the people of Nova Scotia

Distributed in Canada by Burns & MacEachern Limited, 62 Railside Road, Toronto Canada

OUT OF OLD NOVA SCOTIA KITCHENS

*A Collection of Traditional Recipes of Nova Scotia
and the stories of the people who cooked them.*

By
Marie Nightingale

CHARLES SCRIBNER'S SONS
NEW YORK

A-10.71(I)

Printed and Bound in Canada

Library of Congress Catalog Card Number: 76-175930

SBN 684-12680-X

CONTENTS

Introduction vii

The Indians 1

The French 4

The English 7

The Germans 10

The New Englanders 13

The Irish 16

The Scots 19

The Negroes 22

Soups and Chowders 25

Fish 35

Meats 47

Breakfast and Supper Dishes 69

Vegetables 79

Breads 89

Scones, Buns and Doughnuts 101

Pies 113

Desserts 123

Sauces 139

Cakes 141

Cookies and Little Cakes 155

Jams and Pickles 165

Beverages 177

Candies 189

Cures and Tonics 197

Index 205-214

INTRODUCTION

Once more, another Canadian has given us further proof that there is a true Canadian Cuisine. Leaf through this wonderful book. You will see at a glance why.

Those of us who really know traditional native cooking as it is to be found in the different parts of our country are already aware of the proud legacy we have to hand on to future generations. 'Out of Old Nova Scotia Kitchens' by Marie Nightingale will, I am sure, remain part of this legacy. She has shown throughout her book how exceedingly vigorous local traditions are and how they have persisted throughout the centuries.

The first part of the book makes fascinating reading as we start with the table traditions of the Micmac Indians, to the French, English and Scots. The amount of research required must have been enormous, and I am full of admiration for the author. Then come the recipes from women for whom cooking is one of a hundred busy everyday jobs. They embody the very finest traditions of our native cooking. As I read them, I had a feeling of meeting real people who had invited me to their kitchens, to talk of their family traditions — Tatties'n Herrin', Dutch Mess, Slow Pokes, Herbs 'of personal likeness', Poutines Rapees, Chicken Fricot, 'Brewis', Skirl in the pan, Clapshot, Backwood Pie, Spruce Beer, Ginger Beer, Dandelion Wine, to name but a few.

I am proud to have been invited to introduce such a remarkable book. It should be in every home proud of its country's traditions.

MME. JEHANE BENOIT
Sutton, Quebec, Canada

ACKNOWLEDGEMENTS

I wish to acknowledge my thanks to Betty Lumsden who collected and tested many of the recipes that appear in this book,

To Peg Calkin and Tammy Dunnet who read the manuscript, Gloria Beckingham who assisted in the proofreading,

To Ellen Webster of the Reference Department of the Halifax Memorial Library, whose interest and valuable assistance encouraged me along the way,

To Belle Medforth, Helen Anthony, Irene Delano, Lorna Berringer, Bubbles Godwin, Gerry Brenton, and the many others who contributed their family recipes,

And to the Nova Scotia Historical Society from whose papers I received much assistance.

Specified items on Pages 52, 71, 199 were reprinted from Off Trail in Nova Scotia by Will R. Bird, by permission of The Ryerson Press, Toronto.

Specified item on Page 95, reprinted from More About Nova Scotia by Clara Dennis, by permission of The Ryerson Press, Toronto.

Specified item on Page 179, reprinted from Halifax, Warden of the North by Thomas H. Raddall, by permission of McClelland and Stewart Limited, Toronto.

Specified items on Pages 51 and 96 reprinted from Folklore of Lunenburg County, Nova Scotia by Helen Creighton, by permission of the author.

THE INDIANS

In the beginning were the Micmacs, the native Indians of Nova Scotia, and to them belonged the beautiful land of "Kady" — the land the French would call Acadie and the Scots would re-name New Scotland.

Nova Scotia! A land of beauty; of rugged seacoasts, where the waters lash up like so many frothy petticoats in a vain effort to cover the naked cliffs. A land of hills so green as to bring tears to a Scotsman's eye in a nostalgic longing for the "hills of home". A land of beautiful valleys and picturesque coves, tranquil then and now, but which in the interim would echo with the sounds of pirates' soirées. A land to be steeped in the traditions of those who were to settle her — the French, the English, the Germans, the New Englanders, the Irish, the Scottish, and the Negroes. All of these people were to bring their customs, tradi-tions and superstitions to weave the intricate pattern of our heri-tage and change the face of the land.

But now it was "Kady", the land of Glooscap and the people who feared him.

The Micmacs were a tall, good-looking, sinewy race, of a reddish-brown colour, with long black hair and intelligent, pene-trating eyes. Though a fierce foe when provoked, they were, ordinarily, mild and reserved, and were possessed of unusual honesty and a deep love for their mates and their children. They shunned agriculture, preferring the challenging life of the hunter and fisherman, perhaps as much for the sport as for a means of liv-ing.

The search for food necessitated a moving about from place to place. When snow covered the ground living was high, for it was easy to follow the tracks of the moose, caribou, porcupine and other game. Bears were highly prized and the Indians were ever watchful for the tell-tale vapours that revealed the dens of the hibernating animals.

In spring the Indians moved to the seashore to dig clams, mussels and oysters, and with long spears they hunted the wealth of the sea — the shad, bass, salmon and gaspereau, but nothing was enjoyed more than a seal hunt.

Dogs were highly valued by the Micmacs since they were used in tracking game. Only on rare occasions would a dog be killed for food.

The preparation of the Micmacs' food was recorded in the 17th century by Nicholas Denys:

> *"To roast the meat they cut it into fillets, split a stick, placed it therein, then stuck the stick in front of the fire, each person having his own. When it was cooked on one side, and in proportion as it cooked, they ate it. Biting into it, they cut off the piece with a bone, which they sharpened on rocks to make it cut . . .*
> *Having eaten all of it that was cooked, they replaced the meat in front of the fire, took another stick and went through the same process. When they had eaten all the meat from a stick, they always replaced it with more, keeping this up all day."*

There were no regular meal hours. When the Micmacs had meat they feasted until it was gone. Sometimes they would go for days without food, until one of the tribe would bring in a fresh supply. Again a day of feasting ensued with all the braves sharing in the bounty. When their appetites were satisfied, they joined in a dance while the women and children sat down to eat what was left. Women never ate with the men.

"As for fish", says Denys, "they roasted it on split sticks which served as a grill, or frequently upon coals, but it had to be wholly cooked before it was eaten."

Meat was the favourite food of the Micmacs, some of which they smoked and dried in the sun, and stored away against lean days or to carry with them on their long hunts. They also had a great liking for birds' eggs which they ate raw.

For vegetables, there were the wild potato and wild carrot, as well as other roots and plants which grew in the forests. The Indian Pear, or Service Berry, was eaten fresh, while blueberries, huckleberries and cranberries were boiled and shaped into little cakes which were dried in the sun.

Sap from the maple trees was sometimes used as a beverage, but the Micmacs also boiled down the sap in earthen pots to make maple sugar cakes which they considered a delicacy. Roots of labrador and sassafras were boiled to make tea, as were the twigs, bark or leaves of the birch, spruce and maple trees.

The Micmacs held many festivals, including the "Summer Games" at Merigomish. Here they played lacrosse and a game quite like soccer, and held contests in archery, wrestling and foot-racing. They loved to dance and tell stories. Seated around the fire, they would smoke their pipes (the bowls of which were often made of lobsters' claws) and much laughing ensued as the chiefs took turns at story-telling.

But the greatest festival of all was that of St. Aspinquid, the Indian saint who has been called "the grand sachem of all the Northern Indian Tribes". His festival was celebrated annually on the shores of the North West Arm, where Halifax now stands. There was much merriment and dancing, and the menu for the day called for clams to be dug on the spot and boiled to make a tasty soup.

Even after the settling of Halifax, the Feast of St. Aspinquid continued to be celebrated. The Halifax Gazette of June, 1770, carried the following account:

> "On Thursday last, being the 31st day of May, the festival of St. Aspinquid was celebrated at North West Arm at Nathan Ben Saddi Nathan's and at Captain Jordan's, both fisherman, when elegant dinners at both places were provided, consisting of various kinds of fish, etc. After dinner at Mr. Nathan's were discharged a number of cannon, and at Mr. Jordan's, muskets, and many loyal toasts were drunk in honor of the day. At Mr. Jordan's the toasts, after the usual manner, were the twelve sachem chiefs of the twelve tribes, who were general friends and allies of the English."

But the Micmacs were to suffer much from their new-found friends. Their beautiful "Kady" was to be wrested from them, and the account settled in abuse, disease and "bottled devils".

3

THE FRENCH

The first white settlement in Nova Scotia, or Acadia, as it was then called, was established in 1605. A Company of men from France headed by Samuel de Champlain, Sieur de Monts and Sieur de Poutrincourt, set up a post at Port Royal for the purpose of trade and exploration.

Much has been written about this "Habitation" at Port Royal, for here was formed "L'Ordre du Bon Temps" — the Order of the Good Time — the first social club in America. To provide entertainment during the long winter months, as much as to satisfy hearty appetites, the fifteen gentlemen of the Company took turns as host for the day. This meant far more than the preparation of the day's meals, for first he had to "catch his hare".

Each host's menu was largely determined by his luck in the forests which yielded bountifully to his cause. Huge roasts of moose or caribou would accompany smaller game such as beaver, porcupine and rabbits to the table. Waterfowl, ruffled grouse, partridge and other birds added much to these gastronomical meals, as did the fish which could be speared through the ice, such as trout, cod and lobsters. On occasion, when the hunting and fishing did not provide enough to compete successfully with the meals of his predecessors, the host for the day would carry on a trade with the Indians.

Champlain wrote of the rivalry that existed among the group: "All vied, one with the other, to see who could do the best, and bring back the finest game — we did not find ourselves badly off, nor did the Indians who were with us." Special acclamation must have been given to the host across whose path a moose had walked or a beaver had paddled, for it was recorded that there was "none as tender as the moose meat (wherefrom we also made excellent pasties) and nothing as delicate as a beaver's tail."

With dinner prepared, the host of the day, wearing the Insignia of the Order, led the way into the dining hall, while in gay procession behind him followed the others, each carrying a platter laden with food ready to be devoured.

4

When the meal was over and all appetites appeased, the rest of the evening was spent in story telling, singing and merriment. At the end of the evening a toast was drunk "with a cup of wine", while the host handed the Insignia of the Order to his successor. "And," wrote Lescarbot, "whatever our gourmands at home may think, we found as good cheer at Port Royal as they at their Rue Aux Ours in Paris, and that, too, at a cheaper rate."

But this "gourmet's club" was the exception in colonial Acadia rather than the rule, with the peasants sharing no part of it. As a matter of fact, the brave little attempt to establish a settlement in Acadia was, for reasons we need not go into, given up, and our merry gentlemen satisfied their healthy palates elsewhere.

The French colonists from whom the thousands of Acadians were descended came out from France between 1633 and 1638. They were farmers who had a deep love for the land, although they had no desire to spend time on the back-breaking efforts of clearing away the forests. Instead, they chose to settle along the banks of the tidal rivers, building dykes to hold back the tides. The rich, fertile soil reclaimed in this way, was cultivated and abundant supplies of wheat, rye and vegetables were raised.

Of necessity, the Acadians were almost entirely dependent upon themselves and each other. What food their fields and flocks did not produce, they obtained from the forests and rivers. Wild game was plentiful and the streams abounded with fish of many varieties, among them the much favored shad. Wild fruits and berries were gathered, some of which were dried and stored for winter use. The strawberry and blueberry were especially plentiful.

Every farm had its orchard, the first apple trees having been brought out from Normandy somewhere around 1606. From the fruit of these trees came their favourite beverage — apple cider. Spruce beer was considered not only a delicacy but an aid to health, but wines and harder liquors were little known to these early settlers.

From the friendly Indians, the Acadians learned a great deal about how to glean a living from this strange new land. They learned to make maple sugar and syrup and thus were provided with their only means of "sweetening". They adapted their tastes to the wild game of the forest and began to savour the flesh of the beaver, the porcupine and rabbit, as well as the moose, caribou and bear.

On their farms they raised poultry, sheep and pigs. Mutton and pork were salted away for winter use. Their cattle were of a small breed and produced very little milk, so butter and cheese were not in plentiful supply.

Most of the food was prepared by boiling in large iron kettles over the open hearth. Soups, chowders and stews were therefore, the most common fare. Bread was baked in large communal outdoor brick ovens, one of which was centrally located in every village.

The Acadians were a simple people, expecting little and being satisfied with less, so long as their families were cared for. The family was the all-important focal-point; the community, the second. There seemed to be no ambition beyond these two.

When a young couple married — and they married young — the entire community took a hand in helping to get them established. The menfolk set about with their axes to clear a piece of land and build a log house for the happy pair. Gifts of cattle, hogs and poultry were made by those who could afford them. A "feather bed" was usually the highly esteemed wedding gift from the bride's mother.

Thus established, the young couple took up their new life together and became carbon copies of their parents and grandparents. The bride hustled about between the hearth and the wooden table as she prepared her stew in a loving attempt to satisfy at least one of her ardent husband's appetites (a large family was the usual result of the other).

And so life continued, with happiness prevailing despite hard work, until the darkening clouds of political issues drove them from their homes and their beloved land.

THE ENGLISH

The coming of the English was a unique chapter in the colonization of Nova Scotia, for they were to set up their homes in a planned town.

The British government had, in order to attract settlers, offered free passage, free grants of land, a year's provisions, farming tools, guns and ammunition to all who would go to Nova Scotia. And so, on June 21st, 1749, Colonel Edward Cornwallis arrived at Chebucto Harbour, soon to be followed by 2,500 colonists.

In comparison with the Acadians and other immigrants who were to come later, it would appear that the English had a great advantage. Although dense forests had to be cleared and the threat of hostile Indians hung heavy around them, the English did not toil as individuals in isolated areas. Halifax was to be a town with streets, shops, a church, parade ground and a manned fort for protection.

There were hardships of course, for in a wilderness the predominating requirement was hard work. The first winter was very difficult. There were not yet enough houses to shelter the settlers and many had to stay on board the ships, huddled together to keep from freezing. Those on land were not much better off, for the rude shanties, formed of upright poles stuck in the ground and roofed over with the bark of trees, were not enough to keep out the cold. Their only food consisted of the government rations of salt meat and hard tack, and thus, without fresh meat and vegetables to sustain their health, they developed typhus. It is tragic to note that almost one-third of the population died.

But eventually Halifax became a town — a little piece of Old England nestled on a harbour in the wilds of America. The governor and his lady set the social pace, while ambitious merchants joined with the military and naval officers in the merry efforts of "keeping up".

7

The cunning Lady Frances, wife of Sir John Wentworth, perhaps ranked first in distributing a genteel hospitality, for it is recorded that in a single year, she entertained 2,500 guests.

The Royal Gazette carried a description of one such gay event, held at the old Government House in 1792:

"On Thursday evening last the Governor and Mrs. Wentworth gave a ball and supper to the Ladies and Gentlemen of the Town and the officers of the Army and Navy which was altogether the most brilliant and successful entertainment ever given in this country. The Company being assembled in the Levee Room at 8 o'clock the band which was very numerous and excellent played God Save the King, three times over, after which the country dances commenced, two sets dancing at the same time. The whole house was open, every room illuminated and elegantly decorated. There was a room set apart for cotillions above stairs for those who chose to dance them and a band provided on purpose for it. During the dancing there were refreshments of ice, orgeat, cappillaire, and a variety of other things. At 12 the supper room was opened and too much cannot be said of the splendour and magnificence of it. The Ladies sat down at table and the Gentlemen waited on them. Among the ornaments * which were altogether superb there were exact representations of Messrs. Hartshorne and Tremaine's new Flour Mill, and of the Windmill on the Common. The model of the new Light House at Shelburne was incomparable, and the track of the new road from Pictou was delineated in the most ingenious and surprising manner, as was the representation of our fisheries that great source of wealth of this country. To all these inimitable arrangements corresponding mottoes were attached, so that not only taste and elegance were conspicuous, but encouragement and genius were displayed. The viands and wines were delectable, and mirth, grace and good humour seemed to

---

* These were likely the elaborate masterpieces created in pastry and sugar by the confectionary chefs. Many of these ornaments were very grand, some even having working parts.

8

have joined hands to grace some glorious festival. But this was only for the friends of the Governor and Lady Wentworth. When the ladies left the supper room the Gentlemen sat down at table, when the Governor gave several loyal toasts with "three times three", and an applicable tune was played after each bumper which had an admirable effect. At 2 o'clock the dancing recommenced, and at four the company retired."

The inns and coffee houses of the day advertised "hot mutton pies", "excellent beef soup and mutton broth", and catering for dinners could be arranged by appointment. It became a popular Sunday fashion for entire families to visit a tea-house to partake of strawberries and cream — possibly a fore-runner of the ice-cream parlour.

Other entertainment consisted of such summer diversions as picnics and chowder parties on McNab's Island, while in winter, skating parties formed on the North West Arm and the famous Tandem Club had its sleigh drives. Young ladies and officers of the garrison, bundled in furs and blankets, would set off on a merry jaunt accompanied by the jangling sounds of sleigh-bells. At the half-way mark, usually an inn on the outskirts of town, they would stop to enjoy a steaming hot cup of negus, or a dish of sillibub (a foamy light custard made of eggs, milk and white wine or sherry). On occasion an entire dinner would be arranged at the Nine Mile House in Bedford. "Hot turkeys, smoking caribou steaks, reindeer tongues, pickled herrings from Digby, bear-hams from Annapolis, cherry brandy, noyau, and Prince Edward Island whisky" might comprise the meal that would be enjoyed before the return trip back to town.

In the years that followed, the English in Halifax were far out-numbered by people of other backgrounds, but the atmosphere of Old England lived on. New Englanders, with an eye to governmental appointments, developed accents "more British than the British", and adopted the customs of a courtly way of life.

But all this was only for the elite. For the poor, and they were many, life was not so gay. Perhaps the classes can best be distinguished by the way one Halifax mistress purchased her "sweetening". For herself and her husband she bought loaf sugar, for their apprenticed man, brown sugar, and for the poor servant girl in the kitchen only molasses was allowed.

THE GERMANS

Although the location of Halifax was well chosen as a military outpost, there was one decided disadvantage. The soil was very rocky and not easily adapted to farming. Furthermore, the English cockneys were not tillers of the soil, so there was no one to supply the town with food. An appeal for farmers went out to the Lords of Trade in London, and so we see the arrival in Nova Scotia of the Germans. From 1750 to 1753 they came in hundreds and eventually proved to be a good type of settler.

At first they tried to till the meagre soil around Halifax, but in 1753, they moved to what is now Lunenburg, and it was there, where the soil was more suitable for farming, that they proved themselves to be worthy settlers and excellent farmers.

They were referred to as "Dutch" by the English-speaking people of Halifax, the name being derived from the German word "Deutch". Though not always appreciated by Lunenburgers, the term has held to this day.

They were a patient people, the Germans, easy-going, honest, God-fearing and industrious. The women toiled in the fields along with their men, undaunted by the hard labour of hoeing, mowing and reaping. Notwithstanding the outside chores, the housewife kept a tidy home, for cleanliness was, and still is, to the Lunenburger a thing next to Godliness.

Not long after Lunenburg was settled, the farms were producing quantities of barley, rye, oats, turnips, potatoes, cabbages and cucumbers. These they marketed in Halifax along with such other staples as veal, mutton, butter, cheese, poultry and many kinds of fish. Cod, halibut, shad, salmon, haddock, herring, mackerel, smelt, gaspereau, eel and lobster all found their way to Halifax where a hungry population waited.

It was a hard life for these early settlers as they carved their little settlement out of the forests. During the first few years the Indians were a menace and later, there were the added dangers of raids by pirates and privateers. But basically a happy folk with a deep love of music, they found excuses to throw a celebration. There were barn-raisings, flax-breaking frolics and quilting bees, but the most festive of all celebrations was the occasion of a wedding.

Guests lingered in those days often as long as a week, but more usually two or three days. The hostess used to press upon her guests that they must not leave until all the food had been eaten. That took a little doing, since bounteous supplies were laid in for the wedding feast — roasts of mutton and geese, hams, soups, puddings, pies and cakes.

Always there was a fiddler to play his lively tunes for the polka and the Old-Fashioned Eight, or "Stamp Your Sauerkraut". Quantities of liquor were also consumed — sometimes as much as 25 gallons for one wedding!

Another occasion which rated a good supply of liquor was a funeral. Although there was a great display of mourning until the deceased had been properly buried, things cheered up somewhat on the return from the cemetery. A generous table was laid with barley bread and cheese, loaf cake and always a funeral cake, which was a plain cake flavoured with cinnamon.

Although the Germans were loyal to the British Government, under whose sponsorship they made their homes in Nova Scotia, they never forgot their homeland. For many years they conversed in their native tongue, and even now the "Lunenburg dialect" is easily recognized. The traditions, customs and superstitions of their ancestors were held dear and still are a source of delight to "outsiders" — Nova Scotians of different backgrounds.

These superstitions crept into their cooking. Never would a Lunenburger turn a loaf of bread upside down for fear she would upset a ship at sea. It was almost as dangerous to throw eggshells in the fire, but here there was no greater loss than the cake that was being baked.

Simple fare but plenty of it was the preference in food, and many traditional dishes are still made by the marvellous cooks of Lunenburg. Particularly adept at cooking fish, they have become famous for their "Dutch Mess" or House Bankin, Solomon Gundy, Tongues and Sounds and Soused Eels, Mackerel or Herring. Although it has been said that the "Dutch" do not excel in meat cookery, their homemade sausage and Lunenburg Puddings live on to dispute that statement.

In colonial days a potato soup called Kartoffelsuppe, formed a staple article of diet as did certain cabbage dishes, such as

Kohl Cannon and Kohl Slaw. But probably more than any one food, sauerkraut belongs to Lunenburg County.

Always prepared when the moon is growing full, the cabbage would be shredded and placed in a barrel, alternately with layers of salt. When the barrel was filled in this way, the cabbage was tightly compressed with a heavy weight. At one time sauerkraut was stamped down with the bare feet (well washed, of course), but later a wooden stamper did the chore. The kraut, thus prepared, was left to work for several days, and when the moon was on the wane, the brine began to recede. The kraut would then be ready to eat or to store in the cellar for the winter months.

Many songs have been sung about the making of sauerkraut, and it seems fitting that we should include one here:

SAUERKRAUT SONG

Now if you've only listen to phwat we spake about
I'm going for to toll ye how to make that sauerkraut,
The kraut is not made of leather as effery one supposes
But off that little plant what they call the cabbage
roses.

Chorus: Sauerkraut is bully, I toll you it is fine,
Me thinks me ought to know 'em for me eats
'em all the time.

The cabbages are growing so nice as it could be,
We take 'em out and cut 'em up the bigger as a pea,
Me put 'em in a barrel and me stamp 'em with me feet,
And we stamp and stamp for to make 'em nice and
sweet.

Me put in plenty of salt so nice, don't put in no snuff,
Nor any cayenne pepper nor any of that stuff,
Me put 'em in the cellar till it begins to smell,
So help me Christ me thinks it nice, the Dutchmen
like it well.

When the sauerkraut begins to smell and it can't smell
no smeller,
We take it from the barrel that's way down in the
cellar,
Me put him in the kettle and it begins to boil,
So help me we can smell her round for 40,000 miles.

THE NEW ENGLANDERS

There was a constant flow of New Englanders in and out of the province for nearly a quarter of a century. This immigration was eventually to double the population of Nova Scotia, thus instilling into her bosom a deeply-rooted New England atmosphere.

The first to come were the merchants, fishermen, and others who sought to establish businesses in Halifax, but in the early 1760's, they came by thousands to take up the farms left vacant after the expulsion of the Acadians. These farms were situated on some of the most fertile lands in Nova Scotia and therefore, were the greatest source of food supplies for Halifax.

It seems natural that these sturdy Puritans, already experienced in colonial ways, were well qualified to reap a good living from the land and coastal waters. But experience was not everything that had to be considered in their new home. Nor did the peace with the Indians or the banishment of the French resolve all the problems. There was still the severe Nova Scotian winter to contend with. It is said that during the first winter in one township alone, twenty-seven cattle died of cold and starvation, and the settlers were forced to boil hides to make soup to feed themselves.

A vessel from Boston bringing the winter supplies to Barrington was wrecked in a storm, and the settlers' own ships were frozen in the harbour, unable to move. The settlements were miles apart, and each had to exist in any way possible, by whatever means were available. In some localities, eels were speared and clams were dug from under the the ice — the only food to be had during the long winter.

Such seems to have been the inevitable pattern of the first year in a new settlement. No matter who the settlers were, one and all had to learn to face the dreadful winter, which in those days began in November and lasted through May.

But the New Englanders survived to establish their townships all over the western part of the province, which they governed by their own rules. On the farms they grew the grains that furnished them with flour and meal. Wheat, maize, barley and oats all answered well to the soil, although at first only hand-mills were available to grind them. Potatoes and turnips were the first vegetable crops, but the second harvest yielded all the common vegetables — carrots, peas, beans, corn and pumpkins. It was then that the traditional New England Thanksgiving Day was established in Nova Scotia, for the pious planters never forgot that "all things come from God".

Although the women took no part in what is commonly designated as men's work, they operated small domestic factories in their homes. One would think that cooking the meals and preserving fruits, vegetables, pickles and meats for the winter would take all their time, but these proved to be only a few of the household duties of the busy and energetic pioneer women.

They made excellent butter and cheese and in their thriftiness found many uses for buttermilk. Their yeast was homemade, as were their starch, candles and soap. The women also, were the brew-masters of the family and many kinds of wines, including dandelion and blueberry, were stored in the cellars along with their apple cider and spruce beer.

Besides all this, from their looms and spinning wheels came the materials that would clothe the family. At every opportunity they found ways to make light of their work. At the "swift" (the machine used to wind the yarn from the spindle) they kept a rhythmic count as follows: "Here's one, tisn't one, 'twill be one by and by. Here's two, tisn't two, 'twill be two by and by ....."

After the American Revolution, the New Englanders who remained loyal to the British crown were forced to seek refuge outside the Thirteen Colonies. More than 30,000 of these Loyalists arrived in Nova Scotia, of which New Brunswick was still a part. As a matter of fact, it might be here noted that it was because of the Loyalists who settled in Saint John and their discontent with the lack of representation in the General Assembly, that Nova Scotia was sliced across the Isthmus of Chignecto and the Province of New Brunswick came into being. This took place in 1784.

It was quite impossible to feed and shelter the great numbers that arrived. Every effort was made by Governor Parr, but things were so bad that the Loyalists sarcastically dubbed the province "Nova Scarcity." Many moved away at the first opportunity, but the majority stayed to instill further in Nova Scotia the New England flavour.

Of course, the Loyalists were not all New Englanders. Many came from states as far south as the Carolinas and Florida, and hence, to the cooking-pots and kitchens of Nova Scotia, were added the seasonings of southern fare. Butter tarts are said to be the counterpart of the Pecan Pie of the South. Brunswick Stew is another southern dish that is still commonly served in many Nova Scotian homes.

The arrival of the Loyalists brought a new type of settler to our shores, for among them were many wealthy, educated and cultured families. It is said that over half the living graduates of Harvard College settled in Nova Scotia and New Brunswick.

One of them was Brigadier-General Timothy Ruggles of Boston, a Harvard graduate who had held a seat in the Massachusetts Assembly. He built a fine home in the township of Wilmot, where he proceeded to plant his gardens and orchards. It is interesting to note that along with apple, quince and peach, he succeeded in growing black walnut trees - probably due to the fact that they were set out in a very sheltered location.

A letter written by him to New York in 1783 bears witness that General Ruggles was one of the contented Loyalists who had the patience and courage required to make a new beginning in a new land:

> *"Your fruit trees, when compared with these here — I mean apple — are hardly worth noticing. About ten days ago I had a present of well toward a bushel of as fine, fair, sound, high-flavoured apples, as you ever saw at New York in the month of January. Colonel Allen of Jersey told me he had drunk the best Cyder here he has ever drunk in his life . . . Vegetables of all kinds of the very best quality, but not so early as at New York. Fin, scale and shell fish of all kinds except Oysters, the want of which is richly compensated by scallops in plenty, about the bigness of a common tea-saucer and of excellent flavour. The land very natural to grass of all kinds with some of our New England husbandry often producing forty bushels of Indian corn per acre; but am apprehensive from the scarcity of heat and much wet weather it is not the proper grain for this climate. Wheat, barley, oats and flax thrive well here upon the uplands. No bugs ever known in the place."*

15

THE IRISH

How the Irish first came to Nova Scotia is somewhat veiled in mystery. Their's is more a story of infiltration rather than immigration, for soon after the founding of Halifax, a resolution was put forth against allowing Irish Catholics into the Province.

Laws notwithstanding, they filtered in and by 1760, the Irish formed one-third of the population of Halifax. Some of these 1,000 inhabitants were disbanded soldiers and sailors who had come with Cornwallis; others came as indentured servants, while still others disguised their entry by claiming to be English.

The Charitable Irish Society, founded in Halifax in 1786, did much to promote Irish involvement in the welfare of the community. An account of the St. Patrick's Day feast held in Halifax in 1796, lists among the guests as His Royal Highness Prince Edward, Sir John Wentworth, some members of the Council, the Speaker and several members of the House. It would therefore seem that within fifty years or less, the hostility that had at first been accorded the Irish had considerably subsided.

Though not the first Catholic church in Halifax, we would here refer to the Church of Our Lady of Sorrows. This little church still stands in the heart of a cemetery in the south end of Halifax. It is commonly known as "The Church Built in a Day". On August 31, 1842, more than two hundred parishioners banded together to erect a house of worship. Before the day was over the building was "raised, roofed, lathed, covered in, floored, and a great part of the outside shingled". At the end of their labours, these sturdy Irishmen were fed by the women who had accompanied them to the site, and it has been suggested that the meal consisted of "corned beef and Irish cobbler (potatoes), pies with green pastry and homemade foaming beer".

With so much mystery surrounding the early history of the Irish settlers, it is perhaps not surprising that little is known of their home life — understandable, but nonetheless disappointing. It has been said that those in service to the English were forced to adopt their mistresses' ways of preparing food, thereby sacrificing their own cooking heritage. Another assumption is that many who came out later during the Great Potato Famine in Ireland had previously lived so long on potatoes alone, that they had forgotten the art of cooking. This, we believe, is pure conjecture, for though potatoes play an important part in Irish cookery, there are many Irish Nova Scotians who wistfully speak of the luscious potato pancakes, soda bread, corned beef dinners and Irish stews that "mother used to make".

Not all of the Irish who came to Nova Scotia were of the Catholic faith. In 1761, Colonel Alexander McNutt, agent of the British Government, arrived in Halifax with some 300 settlers from the Province of Ulster in the north of Ireland. They settled in Colchester and Cumberland Counties. Soon afterward, other Ulster-Irish families arrived by way of New England and made up settlements chiefly in Hants County. They were mainly Presbyterians and in stark contrast to the Catholic Irish who were forced to conceal their faith, the Presbyterians proclaimed their's in a loud, strong voice.

There are many amusing tales told of these Presbyterian Irish. One settler was asked to attend a Methodist meeting with a friend and he retorted, with not a little disdain, "I would not break the Sabbath by doing such a thing." Another incident was cited by Lieutenant-Governor Archibald on the occasion of the Centennial celebrations in Stewiacke in 1880: "On one occasion at a militia drill, the Colonel was telling off the men in the ranks as right and left men. He came to a young man who hesitated in giving the word 'right' or 'left'. When the officer asked him, 'What are you?' he answered 'A staunch Presbyterian!'"

It was from the same address by Lieutenant-Governor Archibald that we gain a brief glimpse into an Ulster-Irish home at meal time:

> "Then as to the outfit for meals, not much was required. A tin teapot, delf cups and saucers were of course, also wooden handled knives and two pronged steel forks. Two large soup plates, one for meat, the other for potatoes, were all the dishes required for the table. Animal food was used at almost every meal. Indeed the three meals were very much alike. The meat was either pork or beef. Before cooking it was cut into small morsels called bites, almost the size of the first joint of the fore finger, and then put into a pan with fat and fried over the fire — when cooked, it was

poured into one of the plates already mentioned, which, with the potatoes in the other plate, were placed in the middle of the bare deal table. The family drew around, each one helped himself to a potato, peeled it, cut it into morsels, and then with his fork selected a bite out of the meat plate, according to his fancy. Sometimes he dipped a slice of potato into the melted fat in the dish and withdrew it saturated with the luscious fluid.

When there were young children, two or three of them could be accommodated around the frying pan on the hearth. The mother, in this case, has taken care to leave some of the fat and a few 'bites' of meat in the pan, and has sliced some potatoes into it, stirring the whole together, and the children arranging themselves around the pan, help themselves with spoons."

The three daily meals were at first very much the same, consisting mainly of bread, potatoes and pork or beef. But as oat mills were erected, porridge was first adopted for the evening meal and then universally for breakfast as well.

A type of oatcake also came into favour at this time. Made of oatmeal and butter, the dough was rolled into thin, flat cakes, cut into squares and toasted over the hearth. Eaten either hot or cold and accompanied by a glass of buttermilk, there was nothing more pleasing to the children whose "sweet tooth" was rarely ever tempted, let alone satisfied.

The women in these pioneer homes were kept very busy at their chores. There was, for them, the daily care of the dairy. Not only did they churn and make butter for their own use, but enough to send to market. Large tubs, holding two hundred pounds of butter would be slung over a horse's back and carried over the rough trail that was the only road to Halifax.

Besides the baking of bread, there was the spinning and weaving of wool, flax and tow. The Ulster-Irish were experts in the raising of flax and the mysteries of linen-weaving.

And now that we have so willingly entered into the controversy that has long existed about the immigrants from the Province of Ulster, we would like to refer to a life-long conflict that has existed between a brother and sister whose ancestors came from Ulster. "We are Irish" says one. "We are Scotch" argues the other. But the Ulster-Irish-Scotch who settled in this province were all truly Nova Scotians.

THE SCOTS

Of all the immigrants who settled in Nova Scotia, there seems to be no doubt that the Highland Scots had the most difficult time. The Acadians made friends with the Micmacs, from whom they learned a great deal about survival in a strange land; the English and the Germans received rations, weapons and tools from the British Government; the New Englanders were armed with a knowledgeable experience of colonial life.

With the Scots, it was another story. They were poverty-stricken, having been driven from their lands by the fall of the Clan System and the outrageously high rents imposed upon them by landlords. They had no money and few personal effects, other than the clothing they wore. Furthermore, they were uneducated and had the added disadvantage of not being accustomed to the type of hard work they now faced in clearing the land, building shelters and planting crops. Though their very lives depended on it, the axe was awkward in the hands of the Highland crofters.

At first they were forced to subsist on the most meagre fare, digging shellfish and gathering wild fruit and berries. In the spring they picked the young tops of the common nettle and boiled them for greens. One aged gentleman recalled how, as a child, he rebelled when his father tried to force him to eat boiled beech leaves which, he said, his "stomach refused".

Nevertheless, being endowed with a strong personal and family pride, as well as an unmatchable strength of purpose, the Scots accepted the challenge before them and soon improved their circumstances. After cutting the timber and burning it on the land, they planted potatoes among the stumps and were rewarded with a plentiful return.

In winter, they would cut a hole through ice which was often a foot thick in order to obtain a supply of fish. They learned to hunt the moose and other game, the meat of which they froze in the snow, thus providing a little variety to their meals. But they longed for the oatmeal that is so much a part of Scottish fare.

The only bread to be had in the earliest days was made from grain, ground on the quern or hand-mill, but this was so laborious an operation that it was resorted to only when the direst necessity impelled it.

The beverage served at meal-time was a tea made by boiling the leaves of the Partridge berry. In later years, when India tea became available, the settlers hardly knew what to do with it. An amusing story is told of an old woman in Pictou County who gave her first tea party. After inviting several friends to join her in tasting this "new" commodity, she boiled a pound all at once, carefully strained off the liquid, which she discarded, and served the leaves to her friends. It is highly possible that they were content after that to return to their Partridge berry tea.

With the building of grist mills some years after these difficult beginnings, life changed for the Scots, for now they could have their beloved oatmeal, as well as flour, in abundant supply. Bread was now something that could be enjoyed at every meal, and the women began to create their reputation for delicious oat cakes.

Of the Scots it can truly be said that hospitality is a national characteristic. Be it feast or famine, they shared what they had with others and thought nothing of it. As soon as company entered the door, the Scottish housewife would begin to mix up a batch of oatcakes or scones and set her table for a light repast. Indeed, she considered it an insult if this privilege was denied her. No apology was ever made for the food they offered, it being a tradition among them that they always gave the best of what they had.

The "cleilidh" or social visit was a favourite means of entertainment, even though this often entailed a long walk through dense woods with a "fire-brand" in hand to light the way. Seated before a blazing fire, they exchanged a little gossip, told stories of Celtic folklore and sang the old Gaelic songs.

But nothing was so gay as the "Frolic". Almost every chore served as an opportunity to have one. There were "tucking frolics", "spinning frolics", "stumping frolics", "cutting frolics" and other frolics.

According to the chore at hand, these frolics were held either by day or night, but best of all were the night frolics when, after the work had been duly dispensed with, the young folk would dance their reels and "flings" to their hearts' content.

Weddings too, were celebrated with dancing, the fiddler or piper being an important guest. The story is told of one father in Cape Breton, who, after giving his daughter away to her young laddie, was checking on the wedding feast — a huge pot of potatoes and herring — simmering over the fire. "If this is to be a wedding", he said, "let it be a wedding!" and he tossed another herring into the pot.

There are other celebrations that are particularly Scottish, including Hogmanay, the Scottish New Year's Eve, when tradition calls for the serving of Shortbread, and Hallowe'en, when a dish of Forach becomes the central attraction; but of later years, it can be well and truly said that no celebration can compare with that of St. Andrew's Day, when a great fuss is made over the Haggis.

To put an appropriate ending to the story of the Scottish emigration to Nova Scotia, another racial characteristic must be considered — a staunch pride in the land. Even though their story appears to be a sad one, full of the most unbelievable strife and hardship, they accomplished in Nova Scotia what they could never do in "the Auld Country". They became owners of a piece of land. No suffering was too great a price to pay for this esteemed position. Although they were heart-broken in having to leave the land of their ancestors, they found compensation by bringing with them their customs, traditions and even their superstitions.

Their intense pride in their race is sometimes considered by others as being the worst kind of conceit, for who, other than a Scot, could possibly issue this proclamation: "Ye Kings, Princes, and Potentates of all the earth, be it known unto you that McNeil of Barra has dined — the rest of the world may dine now".

THE NEGROES

Since forty-three per cent of the Negroes in Canada live in Nova Scotia, their story is not to be excluded from the account of settling this province. The first to arrive came as slaves to the pre-Loyalists, but slavery did not live long in Nova Scotia. As a matter of fact, slavery was abolished here some fifty years before Abolition in the United States.

During the American Revolution, hundreds of Negro slaves escaped from their masters and sought refuge within the British lines. A large number of them were brought to Nova Scotia where they received free lands and rations and lived as freed men. But they were to find the climate a shocking contrast to that which they were accustomed in the South, so in 1792, most of the Negroes then in Nova Scotia joined the exodus to Sierra Leone which was arranged for them by the Government.

It was during the War of 1812 and the years immediately following that the largest group of Negroes came to Nova Scotia. About 2,000 Negro slaves, having fled from the southern colonies to the British lines, were to become permanent settlers in this province.

The arrival of so many helpless people placed a heavy burden on the Government. Provisions of food, clothing, shelter and medical care were of prime concern, but it was also a problem to find employment for those who could work.

The Negroes, on the other hand, were accustomed to life in bondage and they little knew how to use their freedom. All of their wants had previously been provided for and since they were not acquainted with the rewards of labour, they became bewildered and idle.

Some of the Negroes settled in Halifax and Hammonds Plains, but the greater number were given lands in Preston, outside of Dartmouth. Here a village was laid out in ten-acre lots, with a reserve of 1500 acres to be used as a common for fuel and building materials.

The men were organized into work groups, some to hew

logs, others to cut boards, and the rest to make shingles for battening the roofs. The plan called for two houses to be built each day and as they were completed, other families were brought over to occupy them.

The soil at Preston was generally poor and unproductive but some of the Negroes succeeded in raising quantities of potatoes. The yield, however, was not sufficient to feed the many whose crops had failed, and rations of beef, pork and rice continued to be supplied by the Government. Rice, molasses and Indian meal were favoured by the Negroes, and a bread pudding called Padana was a stand-by.

Many of the Negroes found employment as domestic servants. Some attached themselves as retainers to prominent members of the House of Assembly. The opening of the House was always a gala affair as the coachmen and footmen would vie with one another in their respective splendour. These men took great pride in their positions and always addressed each other by their employers' titles — "Mornin', Chief Justice." "Move ovah, Attorney-General."

The Surveyor-General had originally chosen the site at Preston because of its nearness to the Halifax Market at Cheapside. With a little assistance, he felt, the Negroes would be able to support themselves by supplying the market with greens, vegetables and poultry. The lakes and rivers nearby abounded in trout, gaspereaux, eels and perch, and the facilities were there for the men to use in making laths, shingles, hoop poles, brooms, axe helves, oar rafters, scantling and clapboards, all of which were in demand.

Oftimes, when a man was unable to find employment of another nature, his wife would engage in domestic work while he kept the children and turned out brooms and shingles for the market.

On Saturday, Cheapside became a hive of activity. Country carts were parked wheel to wheel, and the hucksters filled the air with the clamour of their sales promotion. Live poultry added their voices to the din, and the whole affair was a marvellous attraction to sightseers. It was particularly colorful during the approach to the Festive Season, when wreathes and branches, Christmas trees, long festoons of evergreen, dyed grasses and sumach berries were all brought to market by the vendors. In spring, great baskets of Mayflowers and mosses became best sellers, while in summer, wild fruits and berries, ferns and flowers of the woods took precedence.

It is sad to say that today Cheapside is nothing more than a little paved street, and the spots once occupied by carts and wagons now hold parking meters and automobiles.

It would be a long time before the Negroes became adjusted to the winter climate, but they could not be induced to emigrate to Trinidad or Demerara. They became attached to their little plots of land and developed a pride in their status as freed men.

Frederick A. Cozzins, author of *Acadia, or a Month with the Blue Noses,* published in 1859, paints a rather vivid picture of a stop-over he made at "Deer's Castle", an inn at Preston. He described the inn as "a little weather-beaten shanty of boards, that clung like flakes to the frame-work. A show-box of a room, papered with select wood-cuts from Punch and the Illustrated London News was the grand banquet-hall of the castle."

In front of the inn was a swing-sign with this inscription:

"William Deer, who lives here,
Keeps the best of wine and beer,
Brandy, and cider, and other good cheer,
Fish, and ducks, and moose and deer,
Caught or shot in the woods near here,
With cutlets, or steaks, as will appear;
If you will stop you need not fear
But you will be well treated by William Deer,
And by Mrs. Deer, his dearest, deary dear!"

Apparently Mrs. Deer had been a slave in Maryland. She had run away and eventually came to Nova Scotia. Her husband followed her soon after.

In a conversation with Mrs. Deer, Mr. Cozzins encouraged her to make a comparison between Nova Scotia and Maryland. She said she never had to work so hard in Maryland. Her work there had been light and easy while here she had to "grub up old stumps and stones". "Dem isn't women's work", she said, "And de winter here, oh! it's wonderful tryin'. And den dere's the rheumatiz." But when asked which place she liked the best she said, "Well, I like Nova Scotia best." Asked why she preferred Nova Scotia where she had to work so much harder, to suffer so much from the cold and rheumatism and get so little for it, she replied, "Oh! de difference is dat when I work here, I work for myself, and when I was working at home, I was working for other people."

SOUPS AND CHOWDERS

With the advent of the canned varieties the art of soup-making is slowly disappearing, and with it has gone the hearty welcome that was always given to a bowl of savory and satisfying homemade soup.

It was perhaps in soup-making that the thriftiness of our ancestors was exemplified, for any leftovers were tossed into the soup kettle to extract the last morsel of nourishment. Everything in the way of meats not suitable for any other mode of preparation was added to the pot. Bones, gravies that would be otherwise wasted, trimmings of beefsteak that went into a pie, bacon rinds, poultry giblets, scraps of vegetables (cooked or uncooked), bones of roast meat, even the juice that remained on the platter when the roast was half-eaten—all these and more were utilized and turned into a wholesome soup.

When the cook stove moved into the kitchen, the soup kettle was always in evidence. It was pushed to the back of the stove where it could be constantly kept at a slow simmer. Refrigeration was not necessary, for the soup would not turn sour as long as it was kept boiling.

In lean times, when nothing else was available, soup was made from bones alone, for our great-grandmothers knew that in every pound of bone there are five ounces of good food. But long boiling was necessary, counted not by hours but by days, in order to extract the good gelatine that would form the entire content of a nutritious bone soup.

"Soup for lunch" could become a proud announcement rather than an apology, if housewives would again dig out the soup kettle and make use of the bones of roasts and poultry. In the words of one old gent, "She's a real wife, what takes the bother to brew a good pot o' soup!"

Choosing the recipes for this chapter was a difficult task, so great was the variety of soups made in Nova Scotia for at least 200 years. Even the Indians made soup — mainly of moose meat. We were sorely tempted to include the recipe for Moose Muffle Soup, claimed to be a delicious Nova Scotian soup of much renown. However, because of the scarcity of moose muffles (the muffle is the nose) as well as the fact that housewives of today are not the hardy lot they once were and might view with timidity the chore of skinning and shaving the nostrils, we decided to by-pass this delicacy with nothing more than a mention.

Another temptation was that of Portable Soup, which was probably the ancestor of the bouillon cube. But here the stock was slowly simmered for twelve hours and then boiled briskly for another eight hours, *being stirred constantly all the while*. Thus it is rather doubtful that anyone should want to try it. The boiling reduced the liquor and the solid stock was finally formed into small cakes which, when soup was wanted, would be added to water with a resulting "instant" broth.

Portable Soup was sometimes called "Glue" which today might be considered an ill choice of name. Often too, it was referred to as "Pocket Soup" since it was a common practise of sea-faring men and woodsmen to carry the little cakes in their pockets, later to be transformed into a meal when fresh meat was not so handy.

The Public Soup House became an institution in Halifax during the years of heavy emigration from Europe and the United States. It was recorded that during the spring of 1818 one hundred gallons of soup, made from fifty pounds of beef and vegetables, was distributed daily.

Many early cook books contain a recipe for "Charitable Soup" or "Soup for the Poor", one of which was noted as being "fit for the table of any gentleman".

It seems only fitting in this book on Nova Scotia cookery that we pay special attention to the lobster. Nova Scotians believe that no lobsters in the world are quite as good as their own. The favourite method of preparation is to boil them when they are fresh out of the water. However, in the days when lobsters were plentiful and cheap they were served in every possible way. Lobster Chowder was a hearty main dish; Lobster Stew, a tasty entrée; moreover, to get the last bit of goodness out of lobster, housewives boiled the shells to make a soup.

The Scottish Lairds were said to have been raised on broth, accounting for their super-strength and brawn. In very early times oatmeal was used as a thickening agent, but this gave way to barley, and more than ever, the Scots are famous for their soups.

SCOTCH BARLEY BROTH

2 - 3 pounds neck or
    shoulder of mutton
1 cup dried green peas
½ cup pearl barley
2 quarts cold water
2 teaspoons salt
¼ teaspoon pepper

2 onions, chopped
3 large carrots, diced
1 cup diced turnip
½ cup diced celery
1 tablespoon chopped
    parsley

Soak green peas overnight and soak barley for two hours. Wipe meat and trim off fat. Put into broth pot with cold water, salt and pepper. Slowly bring to the boiling point and skim. Add peas, barley and onions and simmer gently for 2 hours. Cool, then skim fat from broth. Bones may be removed if desired. Add carrots, turnip, and celery and simmer 30 minutes or until vegetables are tender. Season with more salt if needed and pepper to taste. Twenty minutes before serving, add parsley and remove any film of fat that has gathered on the surface.

✿ ✿ ✿ ✿ ✿

There are many types of bean soup, for beans were easily kept and were used in every possible way. Even the baked beans left over from Saturday night's supper, if they went beyond the Sunday breakfast table, made their final appearance in the soup pot. This recipe, found in an old Halifax cook book of 1898, makes a very rich soup, so we suggest one helping — at a time!

BLACK BEAN SOUP

1 pint black beans
2 quarts water
½ pound salt pork or
    a knuckle of veal

1 celery stalk
Pepper to taste
1 lemon
2 eggs, hard-cooked
1 glass sherry

Soak beans overnight in lukewarm water. Put them in soup kettle next morning in 2 quarts more water with salt pork. Boil slowly for 3 hours, keeping the pot tightly covered. Add celery stalk and pepper. Simmer half an hour longer, then strain. Cut lemon and hard-cooked eggs in slices; put them in a soup tureen with sherry. Pour the hot soup over and serve.

Split peas were used to make a "Soup for the Poor", the recipe calling for a quart of split peas to be soaked for a day in cold water, then boiled with 2 pounds of "well-bruised" potatoes, herbs, salt and pepper and 2 onions in 2½ gallons of water — this all to be boiled until two gallons remained. But other recipes were employed in making Pea Soup for the family and it was very popular, especially among the Acadians.

SPLIT PEA SOUP

2 cups green split peas
1 ham bone
2 quarts cold water
Savory
Cayenne pepper

2 carrots, diced
1 onion, diced
1 celery stalk, diced

Soak peas overnight. Put ham bone in a large kettle with cold water and simmer 1½ hours, keeping the lid tightly closed. Do not boil. Add peas, carrots, onion, celery, and seasonings and continue to simmer one more hour, or until peas are very soft. Remove ham bone. Rub soup through a sieve and return to kettle. Season further to suit taste, adding salt only if necessary.

۰ ۰ ۰ ۰ ۰ ۰

Today's tastes will probably favour Cream of Potato Soup in preference to the earlier type that used water instead of milk as the liquid. This recipe was served in Government House at the turn of the century.

CREAM OF POTATO SOUP

6 good-sized potatoes
1 large onion
1 heaping teaspoon soft butter
1 tablespoon flour
⅛ teaspoon white pepper
1 teaspoon salt

⅛ teaspoon celery salt
Grate of nutmeg (optional)
2 cups rich milk or thin cream
1 tablespoon minced parsley

Peel and slice potatoes and onion; cover with cold water and bring to the boil. Drain off water and add fresh, boiling water, cook until very soft, then press through a sieve. Rub butter and flour together and stir into soup until well blended. Season to taste with white pepper, salt, celery salt and nutmeg. In a separate pan heat the milk and add to potatoes. Bring to the boiling point and serve. Garnish with parsley.

An indication of how our ancestors utilized in every possible way that which was easily obtained, is shown in this recipe — a rich, creamy soup with a difference.

PUMPKIN SOUP

2 pound pumpkin
1 cup water
1½ pints boiling milk
Butter size of an egg

1 teaspoon sugar
Salt and pepper to taste
3 slices stale bread, cut in small
   cubes

Take out seeds and pare off the rind from pumpkin; cut into small pieces. Put into soup kettle with water and simmer slowly for 1½ hours. Put through sieve and return to soup kettle with boiling milk, butter, sugar, salt and pepper. Bring to the boil, stirring occasionally, and serve.

       ✿ ✿ ✿ ✿ ✿ ✿

This chapter could not be complete without a recipe for corn soup, for corn played its role in early Nova Scotia history. When testing this recipe we used canned corn kernels and tomatoes and liked the results.

CORN CHOWDER BISQUE

2 slices salt pork
4 small onions, finely minced
6 medium potatoes, peeled
   and cubed
4 medium tomatoes, peeled
   and sliced
2 teaspoons salt
¼ teaspoon pepper

1 pint boiling water
6 ears corn
¼ teaspoon baking soda
1 quart hot milk
1 tablespoon butter
1 tablespoon flour

Cut salt pork into ¼" cubes and fry until crisp and light brown in a kettle in which the chowder is to be made. Remove from stove and add onions, potatoes and tomatoes, arranging them in layers. Sprinkle with salt and pepper. Cover with boiling water and simmer until vegetables are just about done. Then add the corn which has been cut from the cobs and cook for 10 more minutes. Thicken the hot milk with butter and flour which have been melted together. Add baking soda and hot milk to the corn mixture, stirring rapidly. Serve hot with toasted crackers.

The German settlers relied on this thick chowder to sustain them in lean times. Some people nowadays prefer to cook the sauerkraut separately and serve as a side dish.

KARTOFFELSUPPE

1 quart sauerkraut	½ pound diced salt pork
1 quart diced potatoes	1 cup flour

Drain the sauerkraut and cook in enough fresh water to cover. Add diced potatoes and cook until soft. Fry salt pork until light brown in color. Remove the pork scraps to the sauerkraut and potato mixture, saving the fat in the pan. Stir the flour into the fat and brown well, stirring constantly. Add the browned flour to the potatoes and "kraut" and stir until flour is dissolved.

✿ ✿ ✿ ✿ ✿

La Soupe au Chou was traditionally served in Acadian homes on Hallowe'en, which was a meatless or "lean" day, the Vigil of All Saints' Day. Nowadays it is often made with a beef stock.

SOUPE AU CHOU
(Cabbage Soup)

2 — 3 pound shank of beef	Herbs to taste
2 quarts cold water	1 small head cabbage, shredded
1 tablespoon salt	2 cups chopped leeks or onions
¼ teaspoon pepper	2 cups diced celery
1 bay leaf	1 cup diced carrots

Let the beef shank stand in the water for half an hour. Add seasonings and slowly bring to the boil. Remove scum as it forms. Reduce heat and simmer for 2 to 3 hours. Add vegetables and simmer for 30 minutes longer.

Eels were plentiful long ago, and to supply variety for winter meals, they were speared through a hole cut in the ice. Some of them ended up in the soup kettle.

EEL SOUP

Skin 3 or 4 eels and remove backbone. Cut into 2" pieces and put in a stewpot with water to cover. Add a teaspoonful of vinegar or a slice of lemon. Cover and boil 20 to 30 minutes or until the flesh starts to leave the bones. Drain; add fresh water and vinegar and stew until tender. Drain again. Add enough milk for a stew. (Half cream and half milk improves the flavour.) Season with salt and pepper. Bring to the boil and simmer for a few minutes. Serve on hot, dry toast.

HOW TO SKIN EELS

Nail the eel up by the tail. Cut through the skin around the body just forward of the tail. Peel the skin off over the head. This removes all the fin bones.

❊ ❊ ❊ ❊ ❊ ❊

The following recipe is very old and had one word, "Excellent" written under it in a fine old script. A little mace and lemon juice will heighten the flavour.

CLAM SOUP

1 quart clams	1 heaping tablespoon flour
Clam liquor	1 quart milk
2 quarts water	Salt and pepper to taste
1 heaping tablespoon butter	

Strain the liquor from the clams and set aside. Boil clams in water until they are in rags. In another saucepan melt butter, blend in flour. Add milk and bring to the boiling point. Add clams and liquor and boil 3 minutes. Serve with toast.

The price of oysters nowadays will make this a luxury dish, but years ago oysters were so plentiful that they were considered to be "poor man's fare", and would be gathered along the shores only when nothing "better" was available.

OYSTER STEW

1 pint oysters	1½ teaspoons salt
4 tablespoons butter	⅛ teaspoon pepper
1 quart rich milk	Paprika

Drain off liquor from oysters except for about 2 tablespoons. Add butter to oysters and place over high heat just long enough for oysters to fatten up and edges begin to curl. (Oysters become tough if boiled.) In a separate pan heat drained-off oyster liquor to the boiling point. Scald milk slowly in another pot to just below boiling point — do not allow to boil. Add oysters and heated liquor. Stir in salt and pepper. Serve immediately, sprinkled with paprika and accompanied by oyster crackers. Serves 6.

✿ ✿ ✿ ✿ ✿ ✿

The following recipe speaks of a pathetic chapter in Nova Scotia's history. During the dreadful winter of 1755, the Acadians, driven from their homes by the English, tore mussels from the rocks in a desperate effort to keep from starving. Long afterward the giant piles of mussel shells re-told the story of these courageous people.

MUSSEL STEW

Wash mussels thoroughly, rinsing two or three times to make sure they are free of sand. Put them in a stewpot, cover and let simmer until the shells are opened. Remove from shells. Strain the liquid through a sieve and, using 1 cup of liquor to 1 quart of mussels, put them back in the stewpot. Add 2 tablespoons butter rolled in flour and a little mace. Simmer until done. Serve on toast.

Nova Scotia is famous for her scallops. The greater percentage of Canada's supply is shipped from our shores. This recipe comes from the Digby area, which is the heart of the scallop industry.

NOVA SCOTIA SCALLOP CHOWDER

2 pounds scallops	2 small onions, diced
Butter size of an egg	1½ quarts milk
6 medium potatoes, cubed	Salt and pepper to taste

Melt butter in skillet and fry scallops on both sides. With a knife, cut scallops into small pieces, making sure they are well browned. Meanwhile, cook potatoes and onions in lightly salted water until tender, but not mushy. Add scallops and milk and season to taste. Bring to just under the boiling point and serve hot with crackers.

✿ ✿ ✿ ✿ ✿ ✿

Although claimed to be an invention of the New England settlers, there is a strong possibility that chowders were first made by the French at Port Royal. The word "chowder" comes from the French word "chaudiere", the type of iron pot in which it was made. The following recipe is more than 100 years old and still makes a delicious meal on a cold winter day.

FISH CHOWDER

2 pounds haddock fillets	8 small soda crackers, crumbled
½ pound salt pork, diced	2 tablespoons butter
1 medium onion, diced	2 teaspoons salt
2 cups boiling water	⅛ teaspoon pepper
3 cups diced potatoes	2 tablespoons finely chopped
4 cups milk	parsley

Cut fillets into 2" cubes. Saute pork until crisp. Add onion and cook until tender but not brown. Add boiling water and potatoes and cook 10 minutes. Add fish and simmer 10 minutes. In another saucepan combine milk, crackers, butter, salt and pepper. Heat just to scalding; do not boil. Combine the two mixtures. Pour into soup tureen or individual bowls. Sprinkle with paprika. Serves 6.

LOBSTER CHOWDER

2 medium sized potatoes, diced 1 teaspoon salt
1 medium sized onion, chopped ¼ teaspoon pepper
1 cup water 2 cups milk
2 tablespoons butter 1 cup light cream
2 cups lobster meat, cut up Butter size of an egg

Cook onion and potato in water until nearly tender. In a frying pan, melt 2 tablespoons butter and fry the lobster meat until red. Add to the potatoes. Season with salt and pepper. Add milk, cream, and butter the size of an egg. Heat to boiling point, but do not boil.

❈ ❈ ❈ ❈ ❈ ❈

LOBSTER STEW

1 quart milk 1 cup rolled cream sodas
2 cups boiled lobster meat 2 tablespoons butter
    cut up 1 teaspoon salt

Scald the milk in the top of a double boiler, or over low heat to prevent scorching. Add the rest of the ingredients and simmer slowly for 10 to 15 minutes, stirring often. Do not boil. Serve hot.

❈ ❈ ❈ ❈ ❈ ❈

The elderly lady who gave us this recipe told us, "If you have been throwing the shells out after serving boiled or broiled lobster you have been throwing away one of the most delicious of all soups."

LOBSTER SOUP

Shells of 2 lobsters 1 cup tomato juice
2 cups chicken stock *or* 1 bay leaf
2 chicken bouillon cubes Pinch of thyme
    dissolved in 2 cups water Pinch of basil
1 cup dry white wine Salt and pepper to taste

Crush the left over shells lightly. You do not have to pound them. Place in a soup kettle and add all other ingredients. Simmer, covered, for 1 hour. Strain and store in refrigerator until needed. Serve hot or cold. Serves 4.

FISH

We have already seen in the accounts of the early settlers that fish formed a major part of their diets. If it had not been for the abundance of the many varieties of "fin, scale and shell", it is doubtful that the settlement of Nova Scotia could have come about when it did.

An early visitor commenting on the hospitality he had received in the cabins scattered along the way from Halifax to Pictou, came to believe that nothing but fish was ever eaten in this country. For breakfast he was served fish and potatoes; for dinner, in another home, he was given potatoes and fish; and stopping at dusk he found once again fish and potatoes set before him for the evening meal.

A letter from Halifax dated August 21, 1749, mentions the market at Cheapside and some of the many varieties of fish that were caught in large quantity:

> *"A man may catch as much fish in two hours as will serve six or seven people for a whole week, such as cod, halibut, turbot, salmon, skate, haddock, herrings, smelts and lobsters; and they lie as thick as stones in Cheapside, so that Billingsgate is but a fish-stall in comparison with it."*

The spawning habits of the various species sent them up the rivers in vast numbers in their seasons. For instance, around Lunenburg County the Gaspereaux came in early May and the run would last three weeks. Salmon and cod came about the end of April, the run of the salmon lasting until the middle of June and the cod continuing until October. The mackerel came in mid-June and were also fished until October.

Shad was the fish most favored by the French and the five rivers in the districts settled by the Acadians literally teemed with them. It was recorded that in 1789, in the Habitant River alone, 120,000 shad were caught.

In the Cumberland Basin where the tides rise to a height of thirty feet, shad-fishing was carried on in a most unusual manner. A ladder was a necessary piece of equipment. The nets, which were strung at regular intervals along the marshes, were twelve feet in height, so that the top-most fish could only be retrieved by means of climbing the ladder which was placed against the nets. The fishermen visited their nets each day at low tide, no matter at what time of day or night this event occurred, travelling by horse and cart over the miles of red marsh mud flats to reach them.

Caught in such numbers, the shad which could not be eaten or marketed were used as fertilizer for the fields. The dog-fish too, though not fit for food, served a purpose once candles were replaced by oil lamps. These fish were rich in oil, a commodity that sold for six or seven dollars a barrel.

Some varieties of fish were smoked and stored for winter use, as in the case of Finnan Haddies and the famous "Digby Chickens" or smoked herring which make a delicious appetizer. The smoke-houses gave up their yield of salmon, shad and gaspereaux as well. The fish would be cleaned and scaled and soaked for 48 hours in a strong brine. Then a good hardwood fire was started. When this was burning briskly, sawdust was thrown on to smother the flames and provide quantities of smoke. The fish were then strung on green sapling sticks and hung over the smoking heap for a period of from two to four hours.

Clams and oysters were preserved for winter use by heaping them in large piles on the shore and then covering them with sand. Re-procuring them was not always easy, for the winter seas would lash up and cover them with ice, often a foot thick. But Nature's freezer, though not always convenient, was most efficient and variety was thus added to the winter meals.

Boiled dinners were the most common fare in the days when all cooking was done in an iron pot over the open hearth. This pertained as much to fish as to the better known Corned Beef Dinners, and there are many who prefer theirs served with a taste of the sea.

SOUTH SHORE BOILED DINNER

1 pound boneless, salt cod
¼ pound bacon, diced
6 carrots, halved
1 small turnip, sliced
4 medium potatoes

4 small onions
1 cup thin white sauce
2 tablespoons parsley, chopped
2 hard-cooked eggs

Soak fish overnight in cold water. Drain and cover with fresh cold water; bring to the simmering point and cook until tender. Drain. Fry bacon until crisp. Combine the vegetables and cook in salted water until tender. Place cod on a platter; surround with the vegetables and top with bacon and drippings. Cover with a white sauce and garnish with parsley and eggs.

✸ ✸ ✸ ✸ ✸ ✸

Kedgeree originated in India from a dish called "Khicharhi" and was probably brought to Nova Scotia by the sea captains who visited far-away ports. Originally a breakfast dish, it is more commonly served for supper or lunch and can be made with leftover fish, such as haddock, cod or boiled salmon.

KEDGEREE

½ cup rice
2 or 3 eggs
1 pound fillet of haddock
    (or salmon)

2 tablespoons butter
½ cup milk
Chopped parsley
Salt and pepper

Boil rice in plenty of water which has been salted sparingly. Cook to just before tenderness. Drain. Hard-cook the eggs, shell and slice them. Cook the fillets in boiling water, just long enough to set the flakes. Strain off the water and break with fork into fairly large pieces. Melt the butter in a saucepan and add the rice, then the fish, salting to taste. Pour over the milk and set over low heat until the milk is absorbed, about 5 minutes. Before serving, mix lightly with a fork, add the egg slices, and garnish with chopped parsley.

37

It is not necessary to clean smelts, but if you prefer, open them at the gills; then draw each smelt between the finger and thumb, beginning at the tail, to remove the inside.

FRIED SMELTS

Take 4 to 6 smelts per serving, or more, depending on what is desired. Dip each fish in slightly beaten egg and run it through flour, preferably whole wheat. Lay the fish in a row in a frying pan and fry until golden brown in butter or olive oil. Turn them over once.

✿ ✿ ✿ ✿ ✿ ✿

Being very oily, eels usually make their own fat for frying.

FRIED EELS

Allow ¾ pound of eels per person

Skin and clean eels. Cut into desired lengths and place in a pan with salted water to cover. Parboil 8 to 10 minutes. Drain and wipe dry. Roll lightly in seasoned flour and fry in a small amount of pork fat to a nice brown.

✿ ✿ ✿ ✿ ✿ ✿

The thick tongue of the cod and the sound (a glutinous substance which lies along the backbone of the fish) were put up in salt and pickle in barrels and pails. Fried or boiled, they make a particularly tasty dish. In a diary kept by Rev. John Seccombe in 1759, it is noted that he had dined on "a dinner of cod sounds and tongues, fried, and cucumbers. A superexcellent dish."

TONGUES AND SOUNDS

Wash tongues and sounds, using several changes of water. Soak overnight in cold water. Put in a saucepan and add enough water to cover. Bring to the boiling point and simmer gently for 20 to 25 minutes. Drain. Fry cubes of salt pork and minced onion until crisp. Add to the fish and serve.

Boiled salt herring with jacket potatoes was a common meal among the fisher folk of Nova Scotia. The herring were taken from the brine as needed and soaked overnight in fresh water. Both herring and potatoes were eaten with the fingers. Still popular today, they are prepared in the following manner.

TATTIES 'n HERRIN'
(Potatoes and Salt Herring)

Soak herring overnight. Next day, clean thoroughly. Scrub unpeeled potatoes, taking a slice off both ends to prevent skins from splitting. Place in a kettle and boil. About 20 minutes before potatoes are done, lay herring on top and cook until tender.

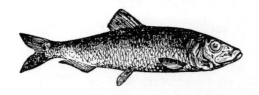

Referred to as "House Bankin" by the Germans of Lunenburg, this excellent dish soon was adopted by the English-speaking settlers, who, unfortunately, found a less attractive name to identify it.

DUTCH MESS
(Codfish and Potatoes)

1 pound salt cod	1 large onion
4 large potatoes	Pepper to taste (a lot)
1 cup salt pork scraps	1 cup cream (if desired)

Soak codfish in cold water for 6 to 10 hours, changing the water once or twice. Pick the codfish apart. Peel and cut potatoes in large pieces and cook in the water in which the fish has been soaking. When potatoes are about half done, add fish and cook until the potatoes are tender. Fry pork scraps until golden brown and pour off excess fat. Brown onion with pork scraps and add cream, if desired. Drain the potatoes and codfish and place on a platter; add the onion and salt pork.

Note: Any left-overs can be mashed and made into fish cakes.

The German name for this famous Lunenburg dish is "Salma-gundi" — excellent as an appetizer.

SOLOMON GUNDY

½ dozen salt herring
2 medium onions
2 cups vinegar

2 tablespoons pickling spice
½ cup sugar

Remove tails and heads from herring. Clean inside and remove the skin. Cut in pieces about 1 inch thick and fillet the pieces. Soak in cold water about 24 hours. Squeeze the water from herring. Place in a bottle with slices of onion, in alternate layers. In a saucepan, heat the vinegar and add pickling spice and sugar. Let cool; then pour over the herring in the bottles.

❂ ❂ ❂ ❂ ❂ ❂

SOUSED MACKEREL

Pickling spice   Vinegar   Butter

Clean and cut fish into serving pieces. Arrange in layers in a baking dish. Tie a few pickling spice in a small, cloth bag. Add to dish and cover with vinegar (or part water, if strong vinegar taste is not desired.) Dot with butter and bake in a 350° oven for about 30 minutes. Serve either hot or cold.

Note: Herring may be prepared in the same manner.

❂ ❂ ❂ ❂ ❂ ❂

POTTED HERRING or "SLOW POKES"

Butter   Vinegar   Bread Crumbs

Clean the herring and take out the back bone. This is easily done by first taking off the head, then pressing firmly on each side of the back bone; pull the bone forward, being careful not to bring the flesh with it. Dip each herring into flour which has been seasoned with salt and pepper. Roll up each herring from the tail to the head and place neatly in a baking dish, shaking a little more of the flour mixture over them. Dot with butter and cover with equal parts of vinegar and water. Sprinkle a few bread crumbs over and bake in a fairly hot oven for 2 to 3 hours. The slow cooking process dissolves the bones.

40

BAKED FINNAN HADDIE

¼ cup butter
2 tablespoons flour
2 cups milk
Salt and pepper

2 pounds finnan haddie
½ cup bread crumbs
3 tablespoons melted butter
Slices of lemon
Parsley

Make a thin white sauce by combining the butter, flour, milk and salt and pepper in the top of a double boiler. Place the fish in a greased pan and pour the white sauce over it. Cover and simmer very gently for a half hour, basting as is necessary. Sprinkle with the bread crumbs which have been mixed with the melted butter. Bake in a hot oven for 15 minutes. Remove to a hot platter and garnish with parsley and lemon. Serves 6.

* * * * * *

BAKED STUFFED FISH

2 pounds fillets
OR a whole fish
2 cups soft, fine bread crumbs
1 teaspoon sage
OR summer savory
1 teaspoon salt

1 teaspoon pepper
1 teaspoon onion juice
2 tablespoons melted butter
or fat
Milk to mix the dressing
(about ½ cup)

Clean the fish, or wipe fillets with a damp cloth. Mix the other ingredients to form a dressing and stuff the whole fish. If fillets are used, place a fillet on a greased pan with the dressing on top, and another fillet over the dressing. Make the following sauce and pour over the fish:

3 tablespoons butter or melted fat
3 tablespoons flour, sifted and blended into butter
2 cups milk
1 teaspoon salt

Cook until thick in top of double boiler, stirring constantly to keep smooth. Bake the fish in this sauce in a 400° oven, allowing 10 minutes for each inch of thickness of fish. Serves 6 - 7 people.

BAKED SHAD

1 shad — cleaned and wiped dry

Dressing:

½ cup shortening	2 tablespoons chopped chives
1 cup soft bread crumbs	1 egg, well beaten
¼ pound chopped mushrooms	Salt and pepper to taste
2 tablespoons chopped parsley	Salt pork

Melt the shortening; add all other ingredients except the salt pork and mix thoroughly. Stuff the shad with this dressing and lay in a greased pan. Cut thin strips of salt pork and lay these over the top of the fish. Bake in a hot oven (400°) allowing 10 minutes for each inch of thickness of fish. When baked, remove to a hot platter. Make the following sauce and pour over fish:

1 cup cream
1 teaspoon cornstarch

Heat cream in the baking pan, add cornstarch and stir until it reaches the boiling point.

❈ ❈ ❈ ❈ ❈ ❈

CODFISH BALLS

2 cups codfish, picked fine	1 onion, chopped fine
3 cups mashed potatoes	¼ cup butter
1 egg, well beaten	Salt and pepper to taste

Mix all ingredients together and form into patties. Dip in beaten egg; roll in bread crumbs. Fry in a good hot pan, using just enough fat to keep them from burning. Turn to cook other side. Serve hot.

The salmon streams of Nova Scotia are still held in high esteem by fishermen the continent over. In the early spring, salmon was a mainstay on the settler's dinner table. As many as a dozen at a time could be taken in a set net. A favourite method of preparing salmon was "planking" in front of an open hearth.

PLANKED SALMON

For this old-fashioned barbecue you will need a hardwood plank about 3 inches thick, 14 to 16 inches wide and 2½ to 3 feet long. A lumber dealer can cut this for you, and it should be kept only for the purpose of planking fish.

Salmon is as successfully "planked" in front of the fireplace as it is outdoors in front of a good fire.

The salmon can weigh from 3 to 7 pounds. Don't be afraid of leftovers — there seldom is anything left, but if there is, it can be used in a salad or a casserole.

Clean the salmon and run a sharp knife along both sides of the backbone, making it easy to remove. Remove head, tail and all fins. Small bones inside can be removed with the aid of a pair of pliers. Sprinkle the inside generously with salt and close for a couple of hours, while the fire is being prepared.

Arrange two bricks a couple of feet apart in front of the fireplace and stand the plank on its edge to heat. When plank is hot, place the salmon thereon, skin side down. To hold the salmon in place, green saplings can be criss-crossed over the fish and nailed at the ends with shingle nails.

Sprinkle salmon with flour and stand on edge in front of the hot fire until brown. Allow about 10 minutes for each inch of thickness of fish.

Serve with hot butter brushed over the top.

BOILED SALMON WITH EGG SAUCE

Wipe a piece of salmon with a damp cloth. Wrap in 2 folds of cheesecloth, drawn into a bag and tied with string. Boil gently without a cover, in salted water, allowing 15 minutes to each inch of thickness. Add two chopped hard-cooked eggs to 1 cup medium white sauce.

White Sauce

	Thin	Medium	Thick
Butter	1 Tbsp.	2 Tbsps.	3 Tbsps.
Flour	1 Tbsp.	2 Tbsps.	3 - 4 Tbsps.
Milk	1 cup	1 cup	1 cup
Salt and Pepper			

BAKED SCALLOPS

1 pound scallops   Milk
½ cup butter   Salt and pepper
1 cup bread crumbs

Grease a baking dish and cover with half of the bread crumbs. Place the scallops evenly over the crumbs and season with salt and pepper. Add enough milk to come to the top level of the fish, but not enough to cover. Dot generously with butter. Melt ½ cup butter and add the other half cup of bread crumbs. Arrange the buttered crumbs on top of scallops and bake in a 350° oven for about 40 to 45 minutes.

✿ ✿ ✿ ✿ ✿ ✿

SCALLOPS BAKED IN THEIR SHELLS

Wash scallops and dry well. Cut each scallop in half. Place 4 sections on a scallop shell. Add salt, pepper and a sprinkling of parsley. Cover with cracker crumbs, rolled very fine. Add 1 tablespoon butter and 1 teaspoon of cream to each shell. Bake in a hot oven, 400°, until well browned.

✿ ✿ ✿ ✿ ✿ ✿

The following old recipe is repeated here just as recorded in a cook book printed around the turn of the century.

CLAM PIE

"Line a deep dish with paste or not as you like; then take the amount of clams to be used, take the hard part of the clam, chop fine and cook for 15 minutes, then add the soft part and bring to a boil. Slice the amount of potatoes to be used (having had them in cold water), boil until half done. Then put a layer of potatoes and layer of clams, a little chopped onion, salt, pepper, pieces of butter, until baking dish is full. Pour over the liquor from clams, cover with pie crust and bake in a hot oven 20 minutes."

In December, 1866, Edward Foley of the Somerset House in Halifax advertised in the "Morning Chronicle":

> "Oysters and Cider. The subscriber has lately received from the country, Wallace and Annapolis, respectively, a superior lot of both of the above articles. He begs to inform the public that meals at all hours can be obtained upon reasonable terms."

OYSTERS ON THE HALF SHELL

Never allow oysters to stand in water before opening for they would absorb the water. Wash the shells and then scrub them vigorously with a stiff brush. To open oysters, insert a knife under the back end of the right valve, and push forward until the mussel is cut. Open the oysters carefully so as not to lose any of the juice.

For each serving, arrange 6 chilled oysters in their half shells, on a deep plate of crushed ice. A small glass of cocktail sauce may be placed in the centre of the plate.

❊ ❊ ❊ ❊ ❊ ❊

SCALLOPED OYSTERS

1 pint oysters	½ cup bread crumbs
4 tablespoons oyster liquor	½ cup melted butter
2 tablespoons cream	Salt (if needed)
1 cup cracker crumbs	Pepper

Drain oysters. Mix cracker and bread crumbs and add melted butter. Put a thin layer of crumbs in a buttered dish; add half the oysters, sprinkle with pepper, and salt if needed. Add half each of oyster liquor and cream; repeat and cover with crumbs. Never have more than two layers of oysters. Bake from 20 to 30 minutes in a hot oven.

FRESH BOILED LOBSTER

Lobsters are cooked live in sea water if it is obtainable. If not, fill a deep kettle with enough water to cover. Add 2 tablespoons of salt for each 2 quarts of water and bring to a boisterous boil. Hold the lobster across the middle of the back and plunge head first into the water. As soon as the lobster touches the water it turns a brilliant red. Let the water come back to a rapid boil, then reduce heat and cook 20 to 30 minutes, allowing 15 minutes for the first pound and 5 minutes for each additional pound. Remove to a platter, claws down, and let cool until able to handle. Serve with lemon, melted butter or mayonnaise.

To open: Slit the underside with scissors or a sharp knife, from the head to the tail. Remove the dark intestinal vein which is greenish in color and runs down the very centre of the back. Also discard the "sac" behind the head.

Although in by-gone days, the following recipe was often served for Sunday breakfast, it makes an excellent luncheon or party dish when served in pattie shells.

OLD STYLE NOVA SCOTIA LOBSTERS

1 pound lobster (or more)	1 to 2 teaspoons vinegar
½ square butter	Salt and pepper
½ cup boiling water	1 cup cream

Cut lobster meat in pieces and put in frying pan with butter, turning the pieces of lobster until each is a good red color. Add the boiling water, vinegar, salt and pepper, and simmer for a few minutes. Add the cream and serve at once in puff pastry shells.

MEATS

As soon as the menfolk of pioneer days had laid in their winter supply of firewood, they set out on some serious hunting. This did not mean the frequent trips into the woods for wild fowl, small game or an occasional moose. Now that winter was here, abundant stores of meat had to be frozen against the time when the woods would be impassable. With enough food including cubes of Portable Soup to sustain them for 3 or 4 days, they set out on snow-shoes in quest of moose, caribou, bear, beaver and rabbits.

Farm animals too, such as poultry, pigs and cows were usually killed in winter when freezing could serve as the "keeping" method. Meat was difficult to keep in summer and if it was necessary to slaughter an animal then, it had to be salted, smoked or pickled.

An important focal point on every farm was the smokehouse, where hams and sides of bacon were hung over a fire, built preferably of corn cobs and apple wood.

Sometimes neighbours would share a slaughtered animal in order to have fresh meat during the warm months, but these occasions were rare and salt meat was more usually the summer diet.

47

Even when the greatest care was taken meat sometimes became tainted, but perish the thought that it should ever be thrown out! The thrifty settlers had their methods for treating meat "too far gone". If it were poultry or game, it was soaked in new milk for 12 to 18 hours before cooking. Other meats were commonly washed in vinegar or, in extreme cases, were wrapped in a cloth and buried in the ground for several hours. But when all else failed, the strong taste of tainted meat was simply disguised by the liberal use of spices.

No part of an animal was ever wasted, and early kitchens hummed with the activities of rendering lard, making sausage meat, puddings and head cheese. Every farmhouse kept a barrel of salt pork in the cellar, to be cooked in various ways when nothing else was available.

Even the blood drained from a slaughtered pig or sheep was utilized. Mixed with oatmeal, milk, suet and seasonings, the mixture was stuffed into tripe skins and hung in a cool place until required. Before the Blood Puddings were broiled or fried they had first to be heated through by placing in boiling water. In some areas these were called Black Puddings, the name possibly having developed as a delicate disguise of the main ingredient.

Meats, game and poultry were not baked until the arrival of the cook stove. Instead they were roasted before the hearth fire. The piece of beef, turkey or goose would be suspended on an iron spit which could be made to revolve for even cooking. Behind the roast was a tin shield which reflected the heat, while underneath, a large pan caught the dripping gravy with which the meat was frequently basted.

Any meats that were not roasted in this way were boiled in huge iron pots, suspended on a "crane" which swung in and out of the fireplace, or fried in an iron "spider" on the hearth.

Many of the recipes for the preparation of variety meats have become rare now that the choice cuts are so readily available in our modern supermarkets. Although tongue and sweetbreads have remained with us, the popularity of the udder has waned considerably. Maybe it can be said that the lack of necessity has robbed us of some of the most delectable foods, for few housewives of today are willing to take the time and trouble involved in preparing some of these intricate and time-consuming recipes. On the other hand, we of the pampered tummies may feel grateful that tomorrow's dinner will not, of necessity, be a Blood Pudding or a Roasted Udder.

TO CORN A BEEF

5-6 pounds brisket or rump
8 cups water
1 cup salt
3 tablespoons sugar
1 bay leaf

6 peppercorns
1 minced clove of garlic
2 teaspoons mixed pickling
　　spice

In a crock, combine and stir well the water, salt, sugar and seasonings. Add the brisket or rump. Cover with a plate and place a heavy weight on it. Leave in the brine at least 2 days; longer is preferable. Remove from brine and start cooking in cold water, in which additional peppercorns and clove of garlic may be added if desired. Bring to the boil, reduce heat and remove scum. Cover and simmer until tender, about one hour per pound.

CORNED BEEF AND CABBAGE: A favourite dish of the Irish. Half an hour before the meat is done, add quartered small cabbages and cook until tender. Serve on a platter with the beef.

o o o o o o

The New Englanders, steeped in the customs and traditional dishes of their earlier colonial home, added much to Nova Scotia cookery. One of their best known "receipts" was the weekly Boiled Dinner. Usually served on Wednesday, the inevitable Thursday dinner was "Corned Beef Hash", made from the leftovers.

BOILED DINNER

4-5 pounds corned beef
6 carrots
6 medium-sized onions

2 small turnips
6 potatoes
1 small head cabbage

Place the meat in a large kettle and cover with cold water. Bring to the boil. Reduce heat and simmer, covered, for 3-4 hours, or until tender. Prepare the vegetables: carrots cut lengthwise and quartered, the onions halved, turnips and cabbage cut in wedges, and the potatoes quartered. About an hour before the meat is cooked, carefully skim off any fat and add the carrots, onions and turnips. Cover and cook 30 minutes. During the last half hour, add the potatoes and cabbage, and continue cooking until the potatoes are tender. Place the meat in the centre of a large, hot platter. Surround with the vegetables and garnish with parsley.

The "potting" of meats and game was a common method of laying up supplies against lean days. Anything that was "jugged" or potted was very tender. In packing the prepared meat into jugs or bowls, care had to be taken to prevent air pockets. The jugs were then sealed by filling to the top with melted beef drippings, butter or rendered fats. Potted meats would have to be examined from time to time in case cracks formed in the seal. These cracks would have to be filled with more fat, before storing in a cool place.

POTTED BEEF

2-3 pounds beef shank
1 bay leaf
1 medium-sized onion, minced

2 medium-sized carrots, chopped
Salt and pepper

Place all ingredients in stewing pot and add water to cover. Simmer until the meat falls from the bones. Remove the meat and mince in a grinder or break into small pieces with the hands. Strain the stock and add it to the meat which has been placed in a bowl. Set aside to jell.

✿ ✿ ✿ ✿ ✿

Spiced Beef was a favourite Irish dish, served as much at Christmas time as the more conventional turkey dinner.

SPICED BEEF

10-12 pound round of beef
⅛ pound salt petre
⅓ cup brown sugar
1 pound salt

½ ounce cloves
½ ounce allspice
¼ ounce mace

Thoroughly mix together the above ingredients and rub them over all the beef. Let the beef stand for 8-10 days in this pickling mixture, turning and rubbing it every day. Tie the beef with broad tape to retain the shape. Place some finely chopped suet over and under the beef, and enclose the meat in a paste made of flour and water. Bake for six hours. When done, remove the paste, but do not remove the tape until ready to serve. Spiced Beef may also be served cold. In this case, keep it well covered so that it will retain its moisture.

POT ROAST OF BEEF

Take a 4 to 6 pound piece of lean beef. Cut a little fat from the beef and melt in an iron pot or frying pan. Season the beef and sprinkle over it a little flour. Sear all sides until browned. Pour in enough hot water to half cover the meat. Cover tightly and simmer until very tender. Add a little boiling water at intervals to prevent burning. When done, remove to a hot platter. Thicken the gravy and pour around the meat on the platter just before serving.

✿ ✿ ✿ ✿ ✿ ✿

Helen Creighton in her "Folklore of Lunenburg County, Nova Scotia," tells the amusing story of Abraham of Mahone Bay. It seems he had difficulties controlling his hunger during the lengthy church services. One Sunday morning before leaving for church he boiled some "doughboys" and stuffed them into his shirt. The minister, quoting from the Bible of another Abraham, boomed forth: "Abraham, what hast thou in thy bosom?" And our Abraham of the Doughboys thinking he had been found out, yelled back, "Doughboys, damn you," and in his rage he threw one at the most surprised preacher.

BEEF STEW WITH DUMPLINGS

3 pounds lean stew beef	1 turnip, cut in wedges
6 potatoes, quartered	3 onions, cut up
6 carrots, quartered	Salt and pepper

Roll the cubed stew beef in flour seasoned with salt and pepper. Brown well in hot fat. Using just enough water to cover the meat, simmer slowly in covered kettle for about 2 hours. Add vegetables and cook about 1 hour longer. Serve with

Doughboys or Dumplings

2 tablespoons shortening	½ teaspoon salt
2 cups flour	1 cup milk
4 teaspoons baking powder	

Rub shortening into the sifted dry ingredients. Gradually add the milk and mix lightly with a fork to form a soft dough. Drop by spoonfuls on top of stew, being careful not to have the liquid higher than the vegetables. Cover tightly and do not peek for 12 to 15 minutes.

51

Another amusing story is told by Will R. Bird in his "Off-Trail in Nova Scotia". It is the story of Penora and Segrim who lived many years ago in Cherryfield. Apparently Segrim had reason to be proud of his wife's cooking and he bragged about her meat pies to his large family. So they came every Sunday, "hollow to the neck". On the fourth Sunday, Penora, quite worn out from these extra duties, was ready for them. She had killed a goat and filled an old iron pan, which is said to have measured 2 feet a-cross, with "Meat Pie". The goat-meat was so tough that Segrim's step-mother "near wore out her store-bought teeth", but Penora had made her point.

BEEF STEAK PIE

2 pounds lean beef	4 cups water
6 teaspoons butter	Salt and pepper
2 onions, finely minced	2 hard-cooked eggs
2 tablespoons flour	Pie crust

Cut beef into ½" cubes. Place in a saucepan and add butter and onions. Cook for 10 minutes. Stir in the flour and add the water. Season with salt and pepper. Cook for 20 minutes. Turn into a baking dish and slice the hard-cooked eggs over the top. Cover with pie crust. Bake in a quick oven for 8 to 10 minutes until crust is a light brown.

❋ ❋ ❋ ❋ ❋ ❋

The following recipe is at least 130 years old and has been served for generations in one Nova Scotia family.

MOCK DUCK

2 pound piece round steak	Salt and pepper
4 cups soft bread crumbs	Pinch of mustard
OR 3 cups dried crumbs	1 teaspoon savory
1 onion, finely chopped	½ cup melted butter

Pound the steak all over. Make a dressing combining bread crumbs, onion, salt and pepper, mustard, savory and melted butter. Spread this dressing all over the meat and roll up like a jelly roll. Skewer together well to seal the ends. Brown well all over in hot drippings, and then place in a covered baking dish. Make a gravy and pour over the meat. (A tin of tomato soup might be used in place of the gravy). Cover and simmer in a 325° oven until tender — about 1½ hours.

VEAL ROLL

Breast of veal Breadcrumb dressing
Salt and pepper Hard-boiled eggs (optional)
Sausage meat

Take a breast of veal, remove bones and sprinkle with salt
and pepper. Cover with a layer of sausage meat and then a layer
of breadcrumb dressing. If you prefer you may put on a layer of
sliced hard-boiled eggs, or some slices of bacon or ham. Roll up
tightly and tie or skewer. Put the meat on a cloth which has been
scalded and wrap it around the roll, securing ends firmly with
string. Put into water to which you may add a few carrots, some
turnips and onions. Simmer gently for 3 to 4 hours. When cooked, place a pan over it and some weights on top to press. Leave
until cold; then remove cloth. This may be glazed with a little
of the stock to which a little previously dissolved gelatine has
been added.

✦ ✦ ✦ ✦ ✦ ✦

*There is a story in the Wolfe family of Dartmouth of a courageous
ancestor who saved the day by her "cool reckonin'". On sighting
a band of unruly Indians approaching her home, Mrs. Wolfe hop-
ing that food would appease the savages, quickly laid out a feast
on the kitchen table. Then gathering her children, she fled with
them to the safety of the barn. Even in those days the way to a
man's heart seemed to have taken a route through his stomach for
the Indians, satisfied with the hearty meal, went away peaceably.*

BOILED TONGUE

Beef .... 2½ to 5 pounds
Veal .... 1½ to 2 pounds
Lamb and Sheep .... Smaller

Boiling water 1 tablespoon salt
1 slice onion 6 peppercorns
2 bay leaves 6 cloves

Scrub the tongue with warm water. Cover with boiling
water and add onion, bay leaves, salt, peppercorns and cloves.
Simmer until tender, about 2 to 4 hours. Drain. Dip in cold
water, peel off the skin and pull out the roots. Cool. Slice paper-
thin and serve plain or with a mustard sauce, or a sauce made
from the stock.

Money was so scarce a commodity to the early settlers that trade was carried on by barter. Even taxes were collected in kind. A poignant story was told of a pet lamb that served to settle a family's tax problems. Amid the tears of the children, the lamb was led away in lieu of the taxes — the sum total of which was 25 cents!

IRISH STEW

3 pounds loin or neck
  of mutton
4 pounds potatoes,
  pared and sliced

4 large onions, quartered
Salt and pepper
1 pint water (approximately)

Cut the meat into medium-sized pieces and prepare the potatoes and onions. In a stewpan, place a layer of potatoes, then a layer of meat pieces and onions. Season with salt and pepper. Repeat in this manner until the stewpan is full. Add the water and simmer gently for 2 hours, keeping the cover on until done. "Shake" occasionally to prevent sticking or burning.

❈ ❈ ❈ ❈ ❈ ❈

ENGLISH BRAWN

5 pounds veal shank
2 large pork hocks
2 teaspoons salt
4 bay leaves

1 clove garlic
1 tablespoon mixed pickling
  spice
½ cup vinegar

Wash the meat and place in a large pan; cover with water. Add the salt and seasonings and cook, covered, until the meat falls from the bones. Remove the meat and cool. To the stock, of which there should be about 8 cups, add the vinegar and simmer for 5 to 10 minutes. Strain. Add the meat which has been cut into small pieces. Simmer another 5 minutes. Pour into bowls which have been rinsed in cold water. Set away to chill but do not freeze. This will keep for 2 to 3 weeks, as long as it is not in metal moulds and is well wrapped.

In the days when men "went down to the sea in ships", it was considered unlucky to mention the word "pig" on a sailing vessel. Therefore, in order to keep bad luck away from the ship, pig was always referred to as "Dennis" or "Mr. Dennis".

TO CURE A HAM

2 cups salt	1 teaspoon cinnamon
2 cups white sugar	1 teaspoon cloves
1 cup molasses	1 teaspoon salt petre

Place the ham to be cured in a large enamel pan or tub. Mix the above ingredients and add enough water to cover the ham. Leave for at least two weeks, turning every day. When ham is removed, rub it well with the spices that have settled in the bottom of the pan. Hang to dry.

* * * * * *

OLD ACADIAN WAY OF BOILING A HAM

1 large ham	2 to 3 medium-sized onions
White wine or cider	Pinch of garlic
5 to 6 large carrots	Herbs "of personal likeness"

Soak, clean and trim the ham. Tie up in a lightly floured, thin cloth. Place in a pot slightly larger than the size of the ham and cover with 2 parts of cold water to 1 part of white wine or cider. Bring to the boil gradually and carefully take off the scum as it rises, and frequently afterwards. Add carrots, onion, garlic and some savory herbs tied in a bag. Simmer gently until tender, about 4 to 5 hours, depending on the size of the ham. Leave in the pot to cool. Remove the ham and strip off the skin. Sprinkle over it some bread raspings (or crumbs) mixed with finely minced parsley.

Note: The old method called for the ham to be covered by a wisp of new-mown hay before wrapping in the cloth.

It was a custom among the Acadians to serve Tourtieres on Christmas Eve and other festive occasions. The following recipe makes 2 pies.

PORK PIE TOURTIERES

1 pound ground beef
1 pound ground pork
1 small onion, chopped
1 clove garlic
1 teaspoon cloves

1 teaspoon cinnamon
1 teaspoon salt
¼ teaspoon pepper
½ cup boiling water

Combine the meat, onion, garlic and spices in a large cast iron or heavy frying pan. Add the boiling water and cook slowly until the meat loses its pink color, stirring constantly. Spread the meat into two uncooked pie shells and top with pie dough. Seal the edges and puncture the crust. Brush the top crust with cream. Bake in a hot oven (450°) for ½ hour. Serve piping hot or keep in the refrigerator or other cold spot until ready to reheat. These pies acquire more flavour when reheated.

✿　✿　✿　✿　✿

Another holiday dish served by the Acadians, particularly on New Year's Day, is Poutines Rapées. They adopted the recipe from the Germans and used it to such an extent that it is commonly thought to be exclusively French.

POUTINES RÂPÉES

20 raw potatoes, peeled
　2 cups or more of cooked,
　　mashed potatoes
Salt and pepper

1 small onion, grated
1 pound fresh, lean pork
OR 1 pound salted fat pork,
　cubed

Cut the lean pork in small pieces. If using salted fat pork, first place in a bowl of water and let stand to remove the salt. Grate the raw potatoes and squeeze the water out. Combine with an equal amount of the mashed potatoes. Add salt, pepper and onion. Shape into flat patties or balls, filled with pieces of pork in the centre. Simmer two hours over low heat. Serve hot with the liquid remaining after cooking, or with molasses.
Yield: 20 poutines.

Note: Poutines may also be boiled. After filling the patties with pork, roll in flour and drop gently into boiling salted water. Cooking time: about 2 hours.

Our ancestors had the knack of turning the hardest labour into fun and frolic. This is indicated by the various "bees" that were the great social events of the rural areas. The butchering of animals and preparation of meats for winter storage was indeed hard work and the chores had to be carried out with the utmost speed. The men of course, did the butchering, while the women kept busy in the kitchen, separating the fat for rendering, the intestines for sausage casings, and the head and feet for "Head Cheese". Nothing was ever wasted.

HOME MADE PIGS PUDDING
(Lunenburg Sausage)

1 heart	A 2" strip of fat from the
1 liver	animal's belly
1 tongue	2 tablespoons salt
2 kidneys	2 tablespoons allspice
Fat from entrails	2 teaspoons pepper
Lights or lungs	1 cup summer savory
(This is all from pork)	4 large onions

Soak liver, lights and fat from entrails in salt and water for one hour to remove blood. Pour boiling water over tongue to permit removal of skin. Cut all meat in small pieces and boil for one hour. Place fat from entrails in a pan in the oven to render out fat. This fat may be used for cooking purposes. When cooked, cool meat enough to handle, then put it all through the meat grinder, also the residue from the fat (this is called cracklin's). Grind onions and fry in a small amount of fat to brown. Mix meat, onions and spices well and if not flavorous enough, more spice may be added to taste. Casings for this may be purchased at some meat packers but if not available, simply fry until hot, as all ingredients are cooked. No extra fat is needed. These are the Dutch or Lunenburg puddings.

SAUSAGE MEAT

2 pounds ground shoulder pork   2 teaspoons salt
¼ pound ground round steak   1 teaspoon pepper
1 tablespoon sugar   1 tablespoon summer savory
                                 2 teaspoons sage

Mix together all the ingredients with the hands, squeezing through the fingers. Shape into rolls about 2½" in diameter, and sprinkle with flour. Chill until firm and well seasoned. Slice and fry. Two or three crackers, crushed, could be added to help hold it together.

HEAD CHEESE

1 pig's head   1 teaspoon summer savory
1 tablespoon onion, minced   Salt and pepper to taste

Cut up the pig's head and remove all the undesirable parts. Soak in cold water for a couple of hours to draw out the blood. Wash thoroughly and place in a pot; cover with cold, salted water and simmer until tender. When the meat begins to fall from the bones, it is sufficiently cooked. Remove all the bones and chop the meat. Return to the pot and add a little more water, onion, summer savory and salt and pepper. Simmer for 20 to 30 minutes. Pour into wetted moulds or bowls and put in a cold place to set.

* * * * * *

FRIED SALT PORK

Cut fat salt pork into thin ½" slices and soak in milk for about 4 hours. Pour boiling water over them; drain, and fry until crisp. When partly fried, they may be dipped in batter, then finished in the same pan, turning several times.

Plain Fritter Batter

1 cup flour   2 eggs, beaten
½ teaspoon baking powder   1 cup milk
¼ teaspoon salt

Sift the dry ingredients together and add the eggs and milk. Beat until smooth.

BAKED SPARERIBS WITH SAUERKRAUT

4 pounds spareribs, split in two
3 pounds sauerkraut

Freshen the sauerkraut by pouring scalding water over. Drain. Place spareribs in roasting pan and bake for half an hour in a 350° oven. Remove from the pan and spread the sauerkraut in. Turn spareribs and place over the sauerkraut. Bake another 1½ hours. To complete the meal, serve with mashed potatoes.

✿ ✿ ✿ ✿ ✿ ✿

In Belcher's Almanac of 1897, it was noted that pork sold for 5c - 6c a pound by the carcass. There was a surplus of pork that year, hence the low price.

PORK LIVER LOAF

1½ pounds pork liver, finely ground	1 teaspoon salt
1½ pounds lean pork, finely ground	½ teaspoon pepper
¾ pound ground fat salt pork	2 tablespoons finely chopped onion
2 eggs	Summer savory

Combine the meats and salt pork in a large bowl. Add the eggs, mixing thoroughly. Add the salt, pepper, onion and pinch of savory. Put in a loaf pan and set in a pan of water. Bake in a 325° oven for 2 hours. Cool before cutting.

✿ ✿ ✿ ✿ ✿ ✿

MEAT PIE A L'ACADIENNE

Chicken, rabbit or pork, cut in pieces	Minced onion
Potatoes, pared and cubed	Salt and pepper
	Biscuit dough

In the bottom of a deep, greased stewpan or pot, place a layer of potatoes. Add a layer of meat pieces, onion, salt and pepper. Add another layer of potatoes. Cover with strips of biscuit dough. Repeat these layers until the stewpan is ¾ full. Add hot water to the level of the last layer. Top with a round of biscuit dough about ½" thick. Make an incision in the centre of the biscuit dough to allow the steam to escape, and cook on the top of the stove for 4 to 5 hours.

TRIPE

Tripe was considered one of the best foods for an invalid, owing to its nutritious and easily digested qualities. Of course, it had to be thoroughly and slowly boiled for several hours, unless bought ready dressed or blanched. When quite tender, it was cut into neat, small pieces and simmered in milk, a little minced onion, a peppercorn or two (according to the quantity of tripe), and a slight seasoning of salt. When done, the liquor could be thickened with a little flour and butter, or not, as desired.

❊ ❊ ❊ ❊ ❊ ❊

SWEETBREADS

"Wash and soak the sweetbread, leaving it in cold water for two hours, adding a little salt. Now boil for five minutes, afterwards put it in cold water to blanch; trim off fat and skin; cut it in pieces, put them into ½ pint of white stock and boil up. Skim carefully, and simmer for 1½ hours. When tender add two tablespoons cream, yolk and one egg, a little lemon juice, and a seasoning of salt and pepper. Strain very carefully and serve." From — "The Helping Hands Cook Book", Kentville, Nova Scotia, 1915.

❊ ❊ ❊ ❊ ❊ ❊

TURTLES IN SHELLS

If you have tiny turtles and wish to serve them in an interesting way, save the top shells.

Take the turtle meat, dip it in egg, then in breadcrumbs and fry in butter. When brown, lay the pieces in the top shells keeping them warm in the oven. Sprinkle with more breadcrumbs, and pour melted butter over them. Serve with sliced lemon.

The National dish of the Scots is the mysterious haggis. We say mysterious because there are many who seem reluctant to speak of the intricacies of this "giant chieftain of the puddin' race", as Bobbie Burns called it. The ceremonies accompanying the arrival of the Haggis on Scottish feast days have modified somewhat through the years. Scots of old would leap on their chairs as the Haggis was piped in and with one foot on the table, toss off a glass of whiskey, following which they would smash their glasses to the floor. Though a wineglass of Scotch traditionally accompanies the Haggis, the lairds of Scottish descent are a little more subdued, and perhaps, a little more respectful of the price of wineglasses.

✿ ✿ ✿ ✿ ✿ ✿

HAGGIS

Clean the stomach bag of a sheep, as well as one of the smaller bags (called knight's hood bag). Wash with cold water until perfectly clean. Then turn inside out and scrape with a knife. Leave the bags all night in salt and water. Next day boil the pluck and the small bag for about an hour and a half. In the process, leave the windpipe hanging over the edge of the pot so that all impurities may escape. It is best to set a saucer under the end of the windpipe to catch the drippings. When it has boiled enough, cut away and discard the windpipe, and at the same time remove any fat or gristle still adhering. Grate the liver and mince the rest of the pluck with the small bag and half a pound of suet. Toast two cupfuls of oatmeal and add to the mince, with two onions, grated, and salt and pepper to taste. Stir in half a pint of the liquor in which the pluck was boiled, and mix well. Put the mixture into the large bag, leaving sufficient space for the contents to expand. Sew up the bag. Put it into a large pot of boiling water, prick in several places to prevent its bursting, and boil slowly for three hours. It is wise to place a small saucer in the bottom of the pot to prevent the haggis from sticking. When ready to serve, make a cross cut on the top, so that a spoon may be easily inserted. Serve piping hot with "Clapshot" (also called "Tatties 'n Neeps") which is simply equal amounts of boiled potatoes and turnips, mashed together, with a large piece of butter and salt and pepper added.

FRIED CHICKEN WITH CREAM GRAVY

Take a 3-pound chicken and cut into serving pieces. Wipe dry. Roll in flour, seasoned with salt and pepper. Brown on both sides in half an inch of hot fat. Do not crowd, but leave enough space for the fat to come up around each piece. Remove chicken when partly done, and place in a baking dish in a 350° oven to finish cooking. Serve with cream gravy.

Cream Gravy

2 tablespoons pan drippings   1½ cups milk
2 tablespoons flour   Salt and pepper

Pour off all but 2 tablespoons of drippings from pan in which the chicken was fried. Blend in the flour and gradually stir in the milk. Cook until smooth and season with salt and pepper.

* * * * * *

The following recipe is of Acadian origin and is a hearty stew. Some recipes call for 1 cup diced carrots, and though this may be a more recent addition, we found it adds both color and flavour.

CHICKEN FRICOT

3-5 pound fowl   1 tablespoon salt
¼ pound salt pork   ½ teaspoon pepper
2 large onions, diced   ½ teaspoon oregano
4 large potatoes, diced   ¼ cup flour
2 quarts boiling water   1 cup cold water

Cut the fowl into serving pieces and the salt pork into thin 1" squares. Fry the pork and fowl until the meat is golden brown. Put in a large kettle and add the onions, potatoes, boiling water and seasonings. Cook for an hour, or until the meat is tender. Combine the flour and cold water, and add to the fricot to thicken it. Season further if necessary.

This fricot can also be made with fresh pork and beef, cut up in 2" cubes and cooked until meat is very tender.

*Curried foods were sometimes referred to as "Country Captain",
since this was a common method of preparing foods by sea-
faring men. There was seldom a sea captain who was not a good
cook, and the recipes he concocted while at sea would be brought
home for his wife to try. The following was a favourite of one
such sea captain.*

CHICKEN CURRY

3 - 4 pound chicken	1 teaspoon sugar
Flour to dredge chicken	1 teaspoon curry powder
Salt and pepper	1 cup water or stock
¾ cup butter	1 cup strained tomatoes
1 large onion, sliced	1 cup hot milk or cream
1 heaping tablespoon flour	

Cut the chicken into serving pieces and dredge in the flour
seasoned with salt and pepper. Put in a frying pan and brown
lightly; remove chicken to a stew kettle. Fry the onion in butter
just long enough to colour slightly. Add the flour, sugar and
curry powder and brown in the butter. Add the water slowly
stirring to a smooth consistency. Add the tomatoes, and further
seasoning if necessary. Pour over the chicken and simmer for 1
hour, or until tender. Add the hot milk and serve with a border
of boiled rice.

Note: Veal or lamb may be used in the same way.

✿ ✿ ✿ ✿ ✿ ✿

*In an old hand-written notebook of 75 years ago, we found this
recipe for Potted Chicken, with a notation: "Grannie's receipt —
very good".*

POTTED CHICKEN

3 cups chicken	2 teaspoons salt
1 cup ham	Little grated nutmeg
4 tablespoons butter	Speck of cayenne

From a cold boiled or roast chicken, free it from skin and
bones, and chop the meat finely. Also chop the ham and pound
it to a paste. Add the butter, salt and seasonings. Pack solidly
in a small stone pot; cover and place in a pan of hot water. Bake
in a moderate oven for one hour. When the meat is cold, cover
with melted butter and store in a cool, dry place.

Probably the most popular of all the Acadian recipes is Pâté
à la Râpure, commonly called Rappie Pie.   It is still served on
festive occasions, and in many homes, for Sunday dinner.

PÂTÉ À LA RÂPURE
(Rappie Pie)

You will need a grater; a large pan, measuring at least
17"x12"x2"; a cloth bag, preferably a small flour bag, since it
must be sturdy and yet allow the water and starch to be squeezed
through.

1 peck potatoes	6 strips bacon
2 chickens, 3 - 3½ pounds each	Salt and pepper to taste
2 - 3 large onions	Poultry seasoning
¼ pound butter	

Cook chickens in a large pot on top of the stove with plenty
of seasoning and onions, before you start grating the potatoes,
so that the juice of the meat will be hot and ready for use.   When
the chickens are cooked, separate meat from the bones and cut
into pieces.

In the meantime, peel potatoes and soak in cold water so
they will stay white.   Grate about 10 potatoes at a time and then
place in the cloth bag and squeeze until all water and starch is
removed.   Do all potatoes in this way.   Do not discard the
liquid from the potatoes until it has been measured, for an equal
amount of the hot chicken broth must be measured to replace
the potato liquid.

When potatoes are all squeezed, loosen them in a large pan,
measure the chicken broth and gradually add to the potatoes,
stirring slowly.   When potatoes are cooked enough they will
take on a jelly-like appearance.   Be sure there are no lumps.
Add seasonings, and stir, stir, stir!

Cover bottom of well-greased pan with half of the potato
mixture.   Arrange pieces of chicken, chopped onions and pats
of butter on top, distributing evenly.   Cover with the other half
of potato mixture.   Then add a bit of chopped onion, more pats
of butter, and a few strips of bacon.   This will help to form the
crust.

Place pie in a hot oven (400°) for about 2 hours, or until a
brown crust in formed.

This is delicious with apple sauce or cranberry sauce.   Serve
piping hot.   Will serve approximately 12 persons.

A Mr. Smith who lived in Hants County in the 18th Century, made it a rule of life not to owe any man a penny when he sat down to his Christmas dinner. He said that this independence was "the best sauce for the goose".

ROAST GOOSE

1 large goose	1 cup water	Stuffing
6 strips salt pork	Salt and pepper	Apple sauce
		Watercress

Scrub the goose with hot soap suds, then draw, wash thoroughly in cold water and wipe dry. Stuff, truss, sprinkle with salt and pepper, and cover entire breast with strips of salt pork. Place on the rack in dripping pan and pour the water in under the goose. Bake in a hot oven for 2½ hours, basting every 10 minutes. Remove the pork the last half hour. Garnish the dish with watercress and serve with apple sauce.

Potato Stuffing

2 cups hot mashed potatoes	¼ cup butter
1 cup bread crumbs	1 teaspoon salt
¼ cup salt pork, chopped	½ teaspoon sage
1 teaspoon onion juice	1 egg

Mix all together and use as stuffing for goose. This same recipe makes a nice dressing for turkey, when summer savory is used in place of sage.

ROAST WILD DUCK

Before roasting, parboil with a small carrot, peeled and placed inside. This will absorb the fishy taste that is prevalent in most wild ducks. When parboiled (about 15 minutes), remove and discard the carrot. Lay the duck in fresh water for about half an hour then stuff with bread crumbs, seasoned with salt and pepper, sage and a little chopped onion. Roast in a 350° oven for about 1½ hours, basting frequently with drippings.

TO ROAST PARTRIDGE, PHEASANT, QUAIL OR GROUSE

Wash thoroughly with soda and water and rinse carefully. Wipe dry inside and out. Stuff with your choice of dressing and sew up. Skewer the legs and wings to the body. Lay thin slices of fat salt pork over the entire breast. Add ½ cup water in the pan and place in moderate oven until tender, allowing 15 to 20 minutes per pound. Baste frequently with melted butter and water. Make a gravy of the drippings, thickened with browned flour.

PARTRIDGE WITH CABBAGE
(A delicious Acadian dish)

2 partridges
1 large apple, cored, peeled and diced
3 stalks celery, diced
2 slices bacon or salt pork
1 large onion, quartered
1 head cabbage, quartered and cored

Pluck, clean and wash partridges, rinsing the inside cavity well with cold water. Season with salt and pepper inside and out and fill with dressing made of apple and celery. Tie bacon or salt pork over the breast and place in a deep roasting pan with onion pieces. Butter the outside of the birds and bake in a moderate oven about ¾ of an hour, or until partially cooked. While birds are browning in the oven, place the prepared cabbage in boiling water. When half cooked, drain. Place the cabbage around the partridges and continue cooking another ¾ of an hour, or until the birds are well cooked. Remove partridges and cabbage to a platter and make gravy with the bird drippings, adding additional water and a flour paste to thicken. The gravy should be dark and rich.

VENISON POT ROAST

This is a good method for cooking the less tender cuts such as the shoulder, rump or neck. Roll meat in seasoned flour and brown on all sides in a heavy pan. Add ½ cup water and cover tightly. Simmer over low heat until meat is tender, about 2½ to 3 hours. Half an hour before meat is done add any desired vegetables, such as carrots, turnip and onions. Remove the meat and vegetables when done, and make a nice gravy.

RABBIT STEW WITH DUMPLINGS

2 rabbits	6 carrots, quartered
½ pound salt pork	6 potatoes, quartered
2 large onions, cut up	Salt and pepper
1 medium turnip, sliced	

Soak rabbits overnight in cold water. Next morning, dry well and cut into serving pieces. Dredge in flour, sprinkled with salt and pepper. In the meantime, cube pork and try out in a skillet. When pork is nicely browned, remove pieces to the stewpot, leaving fat in the skillet. Put the pieces of rabbit in the hot fat until browned on both sides. Remove to the stewpot with enough water to just cover. Simmer for 1½ hours, or until nearly tender. Add vegetables and simmer until done. Fifteen minutes before vegetables are tender, drop in the dumplings and cover tightly.

RABBIT FRICASSEE

2 young rabbits	2 cups stock
1 small onion, chopped	1 cup cream or milk
¼ teaspoon pepper	2 eggs, well beaten
A little nutmeg	1 tablespoon butter
Pinch of mace	Flour to thicken
Herbs to taste	Juice of 1 lemon

Prepare the rabbits, cut in sections and soak in salt and water for at least an hour. Drain, and cover with fresh water. Add onion, herbs, spices and pepper. Cover and simmer until tender, about an hour. Remove from kettle and place in oven to keep warm. Using 2 cups of the stock in which the rabbits were cooked, add the cream, stir in beaten eggs a little at a time, and add butter. Thicken with flour mixed in a little milk. Bring to the boil and remove from heat. Stir in the lemon juice, and pour over the rabbits. Serve hot.

❖ ❖ ❖ ❖ ❖ ❖

This recipe was taken from the "Church of England Receipt Book", printed in Halifax in 1898.

GAME OMELETTE

6 eggs	Breast of a partridge or remains
½ cup butter	of any cold game
Salt and pepper	A little minced onion
	Chopped parsley

Break eggs into a frying pan; add butter, salt and pepper. Fry quickly as for an ordinary omelette. In a separate saucepan combine minced game, onion and parsley, and heat. When omelette is ready spread the game mixture over the top; fold quickly and serve. It must be taken to the table piping hot or it will be leathery.

BREAKFAST AND SUPPER DISHES

In the days when work was hard and hours were long, breakfast was a much heartier meal than it has since become. As a matter of fact, it was not unusual to serve the same foods for both breakfast and supper, prepared in the same way, and devoured in equal quantities and with as much gusto.

On the farm the day began early, usually at dawn, and many chores had to be done before breakfast. This allowed time for the housewife to prepare her fire and get things started before the menfolk came in from the barn — ravenous and ready. And they were not to be satisfied with one course, either. They might begin with stewed fruit, or end with it. After a hot cereal, there was a main dish consisting perhaps, of pancakes, fried apples or potatoes and sausages, cold meat or eggs. Bread, doughnuts, pies and cakes were on the table as well, and the men ate until they could eat no more. Breakfast, then, was a full course meal. It had to be in order to sustain those energetic souls until the noonday dinner.

Pancakes were a mainstay in the old days, being served as often for the evening meal as for breakfast. Buckwheat was grown on nearly every farm, and was processed in the grist mills nearby. The most commonly served breakfast pancakes were made with yeast, since the batter could be mixed up the night before. By morning, the batter would have risen and this left the housewife free to prepare the rest of the meal.

In using a raised batter, care was always taken to ensure that about one-third was left in the pitcher to "mother" the next day's cakes. Every home had a special pitcher for pancake batter and it was never empty. Covered and kept in a cool place, it would not spoil; in fact, freezing pancake batter added to the quality of the cakes.

Accompanying the pancakes to the table were large jugs of maple syrup, honey and molasses, and lots of sweet homemade butter. Fat pork, either fresh or salted and fried to a crisp brown, was a favourite accompaniment to pancakes.

The cold flakes or puffs of today's cereals would find no welcome on the breakfast tables of long ago. But cereals there were — piping hot and nourishing. The New Englanders preferred their cornmeal "mush", and for the Scots there was oatmeal. This does not mean the rolled oats of today, but the standard, mill-ground nutty-flavored oatmeal that has become almost extinct in this day and age.

Bobbie Burns referred to porridge as "chief of Scotia's food" and there are many traditions surrounding this well-known and much-used breakfast dish. For instance, by the Scots porridge is never referred to in the singular, but in the plural. Porridge is "they", not "it". And "they" should be eaten, tradition dictates, while one is in the standing position. This may seem to be rather an awkward procedure, since the correct way of eating "them" is to dunk a spoonful into cream, which is always served in a separate dish.

Probably the best known breakfast of all was the Sunday breakfast, when Saturday night's left-over baked beans were re-heated and served with fish cakes or poached eggs.

A custom that lost favour after the Temperance Societies came into vogue was the "morning draft" of beer, ale or hard cider. With the Scots it was more usually Atholl Brose, and this morning nip was credited with rendering brains and brawn to the already brawniest of men.

Stevens Mountain in the beautiful Wentworth Valley was settled by pre-Loyalists. "One farmer had over five hundred bushels of buckwheat in one crop, and all threshing was then done by the flail. Buckwheat pancakes were a staple article on the menu, and when served with maple syrup made a breakfast fit for a king." — Will R. Bird, "Off Trail in Nova Scotia."

OLD FASHIONED BUCKWHEAT PANCAKES

2 teaspoons dry yeast
1 teaspoon sugar
¼ cup lukewarm water
2 cups buckwheat flour
1 cup all purpose flour
1¼ cups lukewarm water
2 tablespoons molasses

2 tablespoons melted bacon fat
½ teaspoon salt
¾ teaspoon baking soda
1 tablespoon boiling water
½ cup sour cream, buttermilk
   or sour milk

Dissolve the yeast and sugar in ¼ cup lukewarm water. Combine the buckwheat and all purpose flours and add 1¼ cups of lukewarm water. Add the sugar and yeast mixture and set aside to raise. When ready to cook, add the molasses, bacon fat, salt, soda (which has been dissolved in the boiling water), and the milk. If too thick for frying, add a little boiling water. Spoon out on a hot greased griddle. To keep hot and prevent sogginess, place each pancake between the folds of a napkin or tea towel.

✿ ✿ ✿ ✿ ✿ ✿

The following recipe appeared in the New Dominion Monthly Magazine of 1894, as well as in many old local cook books. Although they were probably derived as a means of using up stale bread ends, we found them to be surprisingly good.

BREAD PANCAKES

2 cups milk
2 cups bread crumbs
2 eggs, beaten
2 cups flour

1 teaspoon cream of tartar
½ teaspoon baking soda
A little salt

Soak the bread crumbs in milk for at least a couple of hours. If serving the pancakes for breakfast, soak the bread crumbs overnight. Add the beaten eggs, then the flour, cream of tartar, soda and salt, which have been sifted together. Fry in a little shortening in a hot frying pan.

From an old cook book: "If using an iron griddle, lubricate with a bit of salt pork or ham rind, leaving just enough grease on the surface to prevent sticking."

OLD FASHIONED GRIDDLE CAKES

2 eggs, beaten
2¼ cups milk
⅓ cup melted butter
2 cups flour

4 teaspoons baking powder
2 tablespoons sugar
1 teaspoon salt

Combine in a large bowl the beaten eggs, milk and melted butter. Add the dry ingredients which have been sifted together. Beat with an egg beater until smooth. Spoon the batter on a hot, greased griddle, or pour from a pitcher. Makes about 16 griddle cakes.

✿ ✿ ✿ ✿ ✿ ✿

Blueberries are plentiful in Nova Scotia. In the old days it was wise, when picking berries, to keep a small brush fire going to scare the bears away.

BLUEBERRY GRIDDLE CAKES

2 cups flour
2 teaspoons baking powder
½ teaspoon baking soda
½ teaspoon salt
3 tablespoons sugar

1½ cups sour milk or buttermilk
1 egg
3 tablespoons melted butter
1 cup blueberries

Mix and sift together the flour, baking powder, soda, salt and sugar. Beat together the milk and egg and gradually add to the dry ingredients, mixing thoroughly. Add the butter and blueberries. Drop by spoonfuls on a hot, greased griddle and brown on both sides.

We found this old recipe under different headings — "Scotch Pikelets" and "English Pikelets". The recipe was exactly the same. We made them — and they're good! Try them with home-made preserves for breakfast or lunch, or even as a dessert.

PIKELETS

1 egg
3 tablespoons sugar
1 cup milk
1 cup flour

¼ teaspoon salt
1 teaspoon baking soda
1 teaspoon cream of tartar

Beat the egg and sugar until fluffy. Add the milk. Combine the flour, salt, baking soda and cream of tartar, and stir lightly into the egg mixture. Drop by spoonfuls onto a medium hot griddle. Turn when bubbles appear on the upper side. Serve warm with butter or syrup.

✿ ✿ ✿ ✿ ✿ ✿

A favourite Irish breakfast dish, the secret of success depends upon the softness of the dough, light handling and quick baking.

IRISH POTATO CAKES

2 cups mashed potatoes
1 egg, beaten
2 tablespoons butter
1 teaspoon caraway seeds
  (optional)

1 cup all purpose flour
3 teaspoons baking powder
½ teaspoon salt
Fat for frying

Combine potatoes, egg, butter and caraway seeds. Beat until fluffy. Sift the flour, baking powder and salt together and add to potato mixture. Knead lightly until well mixed. Roll on a lightly floured board to ¼" thickness. Cut in squares or wedges and cook in a greased frying pan over low heat until golden brown. This requires about 5 minutes on each side. Serve at once with plenty of butter. Sprinkle generously with sugar as the Irish do!

Nova Scotia can boast of many giants, particularly among the Cape Breton Scots. Their size and strength have often been attributed to their morning diet of oatmeal porridge. Today's porridge made of instant oats is an insult to the Scots who prefer real oatmeal such as is produced at Balmoral Mill in Colchester County.

COARSE OATMEAL PORRIDGE

1 quart boiling water   4 tablespoons coarse oatmeal
½ teaspoon salt

Bring the water to a rolling boil and sprinkle in the oatmeal slowly, stirring rapidly to prevent the porridge from lumping. Continue to stir until the porridge begins to thicken, about 5 minutes. Cover and simmer for 30 minutes, stirring frequently. Porridge may be cooked in the top part of a double boiler over boiling water and requires less stirring. When half done, add the salt. If added earlier, it tends to harden the oatmeal. **Serves 4 or 5.**

BUCKWHEAT PORRIDGE

2 cups milk   1 teaspoon salt
½ cup water   ¼ cup buckwheat flour

Heat milk to scalding in a double boiler or heavy saucepan. To the water add salt, and then stir in the buckwheat flour. Add carefully to the hot milk and stir occasionally until thick. Allow it to cook thoroughly and serve with sugar, preferably brown, and light cream.

The middle of the day dinner was once the main meal in Nova Scotia. Breakfasts and suppers often consisted of the same menus and Brewis is a good example of this. As a breakfast dish it was served like porridge, with cream and maple syrup. For supper, it would be served with cold corned beef or cold boiled tongue.

BREWIS

1 cup rich milk	1 cup brown bread crumbs
1 tablespoon butter	Pinch of salt

Scald the milk and butter. Add the brown bread crumbs and salt, and simmer in the top of a double boiler for 30 minutes, or until the liquid is absorbed. Serve hot.

✿ ✿ ✿ ✿ ✿ ✿

A newspaper clipping from around the turn of the century referred to the earlier making of Frumety. "For a growing family" it read, "there is nothing equal to this, and if parents would take the trouble to cook frumety, they would do two other things, reduce their bread bills, and improve their healths". The recipe given is as follows:

FRUMETY

"Put one-half pint of whole wheat into a quart stone jar. Fill up with cold water, nothing else. Put a lid on and cook in the oven until it bursts. The following day this will be a jelly. Thin down with milk in a saucepan, cook gently for another half hour. Add brown sugar and nutmeg to taste."

✿ ✿ ✿ ✿ ✿ ✿

An old Scottish breakfast dish was called Skirl in the Pan or Fried Oatmeal. Accompanied by meat and potatoes it also made a satisfying evening meal.

SKIRL IN THE PAN

2 ounces suet, chopped	1 or 2 finely chopped onions
	Oatmeal

Melt the suet in a very hot pan. Add the onions and brown well. Add just enough oatmeal to absorb the fat, stirring thoroughly for a few minutes until brown.

75

AN OLD FASHIONED BREAKFAST DISH

2 cups buttermilk
½ teaspoon salt
1 teaspoon baking soda

¾ cup buckwheat flour
¾ cup white flour

Put salt and soda in the milk, add flour and stir quickly. This makes a fairly thin batter. Have a large flat pan very hot and well greased. Pour in the batter and bake in a hot oven (425°) until browned on the bottom. Serve with fried sausages, sausage meat or fresh pork. Or simply spread with molasses and eat while hot.

❋ ❋ ❋ ❋ ❋ ❋

Scotch Cheese was called "The Coal Miners' Dish" in Glace Bay, Cape Breton. This recipe belongs to a lady in her 90's who, all her life served it for Sunday night supper. Her 72 year old daughter has followed her mother's routine.

SCOTCH CHEESE

Line a pan with cut-up cheese and add chopped onion, using enough to cover the bottom of the pan thinly. Beat 2 eggs with 1½ cups of milk, and pour over the cheese and onion. Season with salt and pepper to taste. Bake in a moderate over (350°) about ½ hour or until the dish is set.

❋ ❋ ❋ ❋ ❋ ❋

SCOUSE
(An old fashioned breakfast or supper dish)

1 pound salt or fresh beef
1 large onion, chopped
6-7 medium-sized potatoes, diced

Salt and pepper to taste
2 tablespoons flour
Water

Dice the meat; cover with water and cook for about an hour. Add onion and potatoes and season to taste. Cook until potatoes are done, adding more water if necessary to keep from burning. Before removing from the stove, thicken with 2 tablespoons flour and water enough to mix to a smooth paste.

OLD FASHIONED LUNENBURG BREAKFAST OR SUPPER DISH

5-6 potatoes	¼ cup butter
5-6 apples	Salt and pepper to taste
2 medium-sized onions	1 cup cream, warmed

Peel and slice quite thin the potatoes and apples. Boil together in the same pot until tender. In the meantime, peel onions and slice thin. Melt butter in a frying pan and lightly saute the onion slices. Drain the apples and potatoes and spread on a hot platter. Over these spread the onions. Sprinkle with salt and pepper to taste. Lastly pour the warmed cream over all and serve at once. Sufficient for 4 or 5 people.

❅ ❅ ❅ ❅ ❅ ❅

STIR PUDDING

¼ cup diced salt pork	1 cup cornmeal
4 cups boiling water	1½ teaspoons salt
1 cup molasses	

Put pork in top of a double boiler and simmer for 30 minutes. Add boiling water and molasses. Stir in cornmeal slowly, and continue stirring for another minute or two. Cook over moderate heat for about 5 hours, stirring the mixture well at half hour intervals. Remove from heat and let set until cold, preferably overnight. Turn out on a platter and slice. Stir Pudding is especially good with cold meats or baked beans.

❅ ❅ ❅ ❅ ❅ ❅

COTTAGE CHEESE

Heat one quart sour milk until lukewarm. Add one quart warm milk and turn into a strainer lined with cheese cloth. Gather cheese cloth up around curd to form a bag, and let curd hang until free from whey. Rub fine, moisten with melted butter if desired, and sweet or sour cream. Shape and sprinkle with paprika.

SCOTCH EGGS

4 hard cooked eggs   Bread crumbs
Flour   Fat or oil for frying
½ pound sausage meat   Salt and pepper to taste
1 egg, slightly beaten

Hard-boil the eggs by placing in a pan of cold water and heating slowly until it starts to simmer. Do not allow water to boil as this will toughen the whites, but keep at this temperature for 30 minutes. Shell when quite cold. Dip in seasoned flour. Cover with sausage meat, then dip in beaten egg and coat with bread crumbs, pressing crumbs well in. Fry in deep fat, (375°) - until golden brown. Drain, and cut in halves. Serve hot or cold.

* * * * * *

SALT PORK WITH CREAMY GRAVY

¾ pound salt pork   4 tablespoons flour
2 cups rich milk or thin cream   Salt and pepper

Cut pork into slices and then into dice. Cook in a frying pan until crisp and brown. Remove the pork to a hot dish and pour off all but 4 tablespoons of the fat. Then add flour. Blend well and add the milk. When smooth and thick, season with salt and pepper. Stir in the pork and serve with boiled potatoes.

* * * * * *

POACHED KIPPERED HERRING

Place some kippers in a shallow pan of hot water. Bring slowly to a boil and let cook for 2 to 3 minutes. Drain well and arrange on a hot platter. Place a small piece of butter in each and serve hot with home fried potatoes.

VEGETABLES

If New England was founded on corn and beans, it can truly be said that the foundation of Nova Scotia's colonization was built on potatoes, for this was the first vegetable grown on the cleared plots of the settlers. Accompanied by fish, the potato was often, in the beginning, the entire substance of the three meals a day. The pioneer story is often embellished with brave tales of settlers who walked many miles to buy or borrow seed potatoes. On the return trip, some of which would take as long as four days to complete, the heavy loads would be carried on their backs.

Once planted, the potatoes grew prolifically, even in the roughest soil. But there were times of famine, when great hoards of mice would swarm over the countryside eating everything in their path. The worst of these plagues was in 1815, which has since been referred to as "The Year of the Mice".

Other staples were turnips and cabbages. At harvest time cabbages were uprooted and turned heads down in the fields, to be covered with snow and thus frozen until required for use. It was not unusual, particularly along the South Shore, to find single cabbages weighing up to twenty-five pounds.

Two early visitors from England recorded "an abundance of cucumbers, the largest we ever saw." They further noted that "what vegetables of any kind once began to grow, they make a more rapid progress than any we observed in England".

An even earlier account pertaining to the fertility of Nova Scotia soil, was sent to Paris by Charlebois in the 17th century: "Near the harbour of La Have, one single grain of wheat produced 150 ears of corn, each of them so loaded with grain that they were forced to enclose all the ears in a ring of iron and support them with a pole; and near the same place there was a field of wheat where every one of which had an ear at least half a foot long."

It was not until the arrival of the New Englanders that beans became an important commodity. The Micmacs were not farmers and the Acadians were satisfied with the broad beans and lima beans which were popular in Europe. So it was the New Englanders who introduced into Nova Scotia the Saturday night supper of baked beans and brown bread, a time-honoured tradition that still lingers in many country homes.

The use of corn and cornmeal must also be credited to the New Englanders. In his "History of Bridgetown", John Irvin gives us an interesting description of an evening meal:

> In winter the evening meal was partaken of quite early, usually about 5 o'clock. A favourite dish at this meal was composed of Indian cornmeal, boiled with milk, which was called 'saupon'. Its excellence consisted not so much in its ingredients as in the manner of its preparation, which began immediately after the dinner. A goodly sized pot was nearly filled with sweet milk; into this was stirred meal made from home-grown corn sufficient to make a stiff batter, seasoned with salt. The pot was then hung on the crane over the fire, and allowed to boil and bubble all the afternoon till teatime. It was then served with sugar and cream or milk. This with bread, made from wheat grown on the farm, carriway seed biscuit, freshly baked and home-made cheese, with milk as a drink for the younger members of the family, and a great dish of tea for the seniors, comprized the evening meal."

Apart from the vegetables grown by cultivation, the forests and wilds provided a wealth of greens. Fiddleheads, an edible portion of the ostrich fern, were picked in the spring and served as a cooked vegetable, as were dandelion greens, sour dock, sheep's sorrel and lamb's quarters. Wild goose grass and other marsh grasses were used as much for a spring tonic as for a vegetable. Dulse, a type of seaweed which is harvested from the rocks at low tide and spread on the grass to dry, is even today a popular treat. However, it is rather sad to realize that more and more children are satisfying their between-meal-hunger with bags of potato chips, rather than with delicious Nova Scotia dulse, abounding in health-giving properties.

BAKED BEANS

1 pound dried beans	1 teaspoon salt
½ tablespoon dry mustard	⅛ teaspoon pepper
⅓ cup brown sugar	1 pound diced, salt pork
¼ cup molasses	1 medium onion

Soak beans overnight in plenty of water to cover. The next day, parboil gently for 1½ hours. Drain and place in bean crock with mustard, sugar, molasses, salt, pepper and salt pork. Stir well and add just enough water to cover. Place the onion on top and bake in a slow oven (300°) for 6 to 8 hours, covered. Add boiling water two or three times to keep beans moist. Uncover the last hour to brown, if desired. Do not add water during the last hour.

* * * * * *

HODGE PODGE
(A dinner of new vegetables)

String beans	Cauliflower
Carrots	1 cup diced, salt pork
Potatoes	1 cup cream
Peas	Chives

Prepare new vegetables. The string beans, carrots and potatoes may be cooked together in boiling, salted water. Cook the peas and cauliflower separately. Fry the salt pork to a golden brown, and add the cream and an equal amount of vegetable stock. Season with chives. Bring to the boil quickly and serve over the vegetables.

* * * * * *

BEAN HODGE

Fresh green beans	Salt and pepper
Salt pork	

Wash and break green beans into one-inch pieces. Cook in a small amount of water with a medium-sized piece of salt pork, about 20 to 30 minutes. Season with salt and pepper. New small potatoes may be added when the beans are half cooked, if desired.

In the old days both dried beans and dried corn were used to make succotash, and after soaking overnight, 2 hours of cooking time was required.

WINTER SUCCOTASH

1 cup lima beans	1 tablespoon melted butter
2 quarts cold water	1 tablespoon flour
½ pound salt pork	Salt and pepper to taste
1 can corn	1 cup cream (if desired)

Parboil the beans, then put in a kettle with the cold water and salt pork. (¼ pound of butter may be used instead of the pork). Cook for 3 hours, then add the corn, melted butter and flour. Cook ¾ of an hour longer. Season with salt and pepper. Heat the cream and add just before serving.

✻ ✻ ✻ ✻ ✻ ✻

SUMMER SUCCOTASH

1 quart shelled, yellow eye beans	1 tablespoon melted butter
	1 tablespoon flour
9 - 10 ears corn	Salt and pepper to taste
1 quart water	1 cup cream (if desired)
½ pound salt pork	

Cut the corn off the cobs and put cobs in cold water with the beans. Cook until the sweetness is out of the cobs. Remove, add the salt pork to the beans and continue cooking. Add the corn kernels and cook until beans and corn are tender. About ½ hour before serving, add the melted butter, flour, salt and pepper. Heat the cream and add just before serving. Use more butter if cream is not used.

✻ ✻ ✻ ✻ ✻ ✻

SANDFIRE GREENS

In early spring these greens appear on the fertile marshes of the Bay of Fundy and are delicious.

Cut off the roots and wash well. Cook until tender in small amount of water. Cool enough so that they can be handled, and remove woody centres by grasping stem and pulling gently. Reheat with butter. Add a few drops of vinegar, if desired.

Fiddleheads are young fern leaves. They are picked in the early spring before they unfold, when they resemble fiddle or violin heads in appearance, hence their name. For generations in the Maritimes, they have been used as the first spring greens. They are tedious to clean but sweet to eat.

FIDDLEHEADS

Clean, then wash fiddleheads thoroughly, giving them several rinsings. Place in a saucepan over low heat and cook for 10 to 15 minutes, covered. Do not add any more water than what clings to them from the rinsings. They must not overcook, so watch them closely while cooking. Serve with salt, pepper, butter and a sprinkling of vinegar.

✿ ✿ ✿ ✿ ✿ ✿

Dandelions were considered to be a natural spring tonic and were dug up in the spring before the buds had opened.

DANDELION GREENS

Remove the brown leaves and roots of the dandelions and wash in at least three waters. Let soak overnight in cold water. Cook in a small amount of boiling salted water, to which a pinch of baking soda is added when the boiling point is reached. Simmer greens about 1 hour, then drain well and serve with lemon juice, vinegar, or the fat from fried salt pork.

✿ ✿ ✿ ✿ ✿ ✿

Another green that is still gathered and served in Nova Scotia goes by the odd name of Lamb's Quarters. It grows wild in the gardens, and those who don't know of its delicacy toss it aside as a weed.

LAMB'S QUARTERS

Salt and pepper   Butter   1 lemon, sliced

Wash the leaves well, and place in a pot without further water being added than what has remained after rinsing. Cover and cook about 10 minutes over medium heat. Drain thoroughly. Season with salt and pepper, dot with butter, and serve with a lemon slice.

Kohl Slaw is a favourite German dish frequently served with roast turkey, spareribs and sausages. In the old days large helpings sometimes constituted the entire main course of a meal.

KOHL SLAW

1 head cabbage, chopped fine	¼ cup butter
½ cup vinegar	or ½ pound fat pork
½ cup brown sugar	Salt and pepper

Put vinegar, sugar and butter in a good-sized pot. Add cabbage, salt and pepper. Cook on top of stove about ¾ of an hour, until cabbage is tender.

✿ ✿ ✿ ✿ ✿ ✿

Kohl Cannon is made in various ways. The Irish simply use mashed potatoes, cooked cabbage and onion, while the Lunenburg Germans like to include turnip and pork scraps, with the pork scraps being removed before serving. The Scots added carrots. But no matter how it was made the eating of Kohl Cannon was a common custom on Hallowe'en. In it would be buried a penny, a match, a ring and a button, all well wrapped (it is hoped) in waxed paper. These favours would signify marriage, spinsterhood, money or poverty, respectively, and much excitement was aroused, especially among the young maidens who were hopeful that the Kohl Cannon would foretell their future happiness.

KOHL CANNON or COLCANNON

1 head cabbage	½ cup butter
1 small turnip	Salt and pepper to taste
5 medium-sized potatoes	

Cook cabbage and turnip for about 45 minutes. Add potatoes which have been sliced, and cook until tender. Drain and mash all together. Add butter and season with salt and pepper.

CREAMED CABBAGE
(Cape Breton Style)

1 small cabbage
1 teaspoon salt
Pinch of pepper
Little vinegar

Butter
1 egg
1 cup cream

Cut up cabbage and cook until tender in small amount of water. Cabbage should be almost dry when done. Season with salt, pepper, vinegar and butter. Beat egg and add the cream. Stir egg mixture quickly into the cabbage before removing from stove. Do not allow to boil after the cream has been added, as it will curdle.

✿ ✿ ✿ ✿ ✿ ✿

CUCUMBERS WITH SOUR CREAM
(A delicious old Lunenburg dish)

3 to 4 cucumbers
Salt
1 onion, finely chopped

1 cup sour cream
1 tablespoon vinegar
3 tablespoons sugar
Pepper

Peel cucumbers and slice thinly. Put in a bowl and sprinkle with salt. Add onion if desired. Put a saucer on top and press with a weight for several hours. This removes the juice from the cucumbers. Pour off juice and mix cucumbers with a dressing made of sour cream, vinegar, sugar and pepper. Pour over cucumbers and blend thoroughly.

✿ ✿ ✿ ✿ ✿ ✿

DIKE MUSHROOMS

Dike mushrooms were plentiful along the Fundy Shore and were there for the picking. They were simply sauted in butter or creamed and served on toast as a favourite supper dish.

For a long time tomatoes were thought to be poisonous. This belief, however, must have been passe by 1860, for in a Godey's Lady's Book of that year it is referred to as a "delicious and wholesome vegetable". It also states that tomatoes should "always be cooked for three hours", so we assume that even then, tomatoes were in the early stages of experimentation. The following recipe was used around the turn of the century.

STUFFED TOMATOES

6 medium-sized tomatoes
Salt
2 tablespoons butter
½ tablespoon onion, finely
   chopped

½ cup soft, stale bread crumbs
½ cup cold, cooked chicken
1 egg, beaten
1 cup buttered bread crumbs

Wipe and remove stem ends and a thin slice off the top of tomatoes. Remove seeds and some of the pulp. Sprinkle inside of tomatoes with salt; invert and let stand half an hour. Cook the butter and onions together for 5 minutes, stirring constantly. Add bread crumbs, chicken, tomato pulp, and salt and pepper to taste. Cook a further 5 minutes. Add the beaten egg and cook one more minute. Refill tomatoes with this mixture. Sprinkle with buttered bread crumbs and bake in a 375° oven for 20 minutes.

✿ ✿ ✿ ✿ ✿ ✿

FRIED GREEN TOMATOES

Tomatoes, sliced
Flour

Salt and pepper
Bacon fat

Dredge green tomato slices with flour; season with salt and pepper and fry until browned, about 10 minutes, in bacon fat.

An old Scottish favourite, these potatoes are cooked on top of the stove.

STOVIES
(Scotch Stoved Potatoes)

6 medium-sized potatoes   ¼ cup beef drippings,
2 medium-sized onions   bacon fat or butter
Salt and pepper   1 cup water or stock

Peel potatoes and onions and slice in alternate layers into a heavy saucepan. Season each layer. Dot with fat. Add a cup of water or stock and simmer, covered, on low heat for 30 minutes, or until potatoes are tender and most of the liquid is absorbed.

❀ ❀ ❀ ❀ ❀ ❀

FRICASSED POTATOES
(An old Irish recipe)

2 tablespoons butter   Salt and pepper
1 cup cream or rich milk   Boiled potatoes, cold and sliced

Melt butter in a saucepan. Add the cream and season with salt and pepper. Bring to the simmering point and add potatoes. Put in a 375° - 400° oven and brown the potatoes on top.

❀ ❀ ❀ ❀ ❀ ❀

CHAMP
(A common Irish dish, sometimes called Chappit Tatties)

1½ pounds potatoes   Salt and pepper
½ pint hot milk   Butter

Peel potatoes and cook in salted water until tender. Drain, then tilt the lid until the potatoes "dry off". Mash, add salt, pepper, and milk and beat until smooth. Serve on individual plates. Make a hole in the centre of the Champ and place in it a large piece of butter. Then dip each forkful into the melting butter, when eating.

CLAPSHOT or TATTIES 'N NEEPS

The Scot's way of using up left-over mashed potatoes and turnips.

Mix equal amounts of mashed potatoes and mashed turnips with a little hot water or hot milk. Heat in top of double boiler and season to taste. When hot, put a large piece of butter into the centre and stir in.

✿ ✿ ✿ ✿ ✿ ✿

STUFFED CAULIFLOWER
(A Halifax recipe of 1898)

Boil the cauliflower whole, until cooked but not so soft that it can be pulled to pieces. With a sharp knife remove a small part of the heart of the flower. Make a stuffing of the chopped cauliflower heart and 3 or 4 cooked mushrooms, seasoned with cayenne. Make a good white sauce and mix in some Parmesan cheese. Pour this sauce over the cauliflower and serve very hot.

✿ ✿ ✿ ✿ ✿ ✿

CORN ON THE COB

Choose the freshest corn possible. Nothing is so delicious as corn pulled directly from the stalk. (To test the freshness and tenderness of corn break a kernel with your nail. If the milk spurts out it is young and tender.) Husk the corn and remove the silk. Have a large kettle of boiling water ready. Drop in the corn, making sure there is enough water to completely cover. For very young corn, boil from 4 to 6 minutes. Longer boiling is necessary for older corn, about 10 minutes. Test with a fork for tenderness. Drain and serve immediately with salt and lots of butter.

Note: Never add salt or sugar to the water in which the corn is boiled for this causes the corn to shrivel.

BREADS

The first bread in Nova Scotia was made by the French at Port Royal in 1605, the Micmacs never having known its taste until the coming of the white man. It has been said that when the French tried to teach the Indians the art of bread-making they showed no interest in the tedious labour of grinding the corn. Though they gladly accepted prepared loaves as gifts and barter they, the Indians, continued to boil the corn whole. This, of course, resulted in a "mush" rather than anything that could be termed bread.

One of the earliest methods of making bread was to cook it in the hot sand after the live coals had been scraped away. The top of the dough was covered with more hot sand to insure that it would be cooked through. In some localities bread was baked in this way as late as 1890.

The French, as we have already seen, baked their bread in large outdoor ovens. Although the long loaf that has become familiar to us as French bread was a product of the 17th century in France, the loaves of the Acadians were round in shape.

Through the writings of an early visitor to Nova Scotia we are privileged to see a pre-Loyalist housewife 'at work preparing her bread:

"After kneading the dough, the landlady formed

89

it into a beautiful large cake of an oval form, nearly an inch thick, swept a part of the hearth clean, and there laid it flat. She then spread over it a thin layer of fine cold ashes, and over that a thick layer of hot ashes, mixed with burning coals. By the time the tea-kettle boiled, the bread was baked. The landlady with the fire-shovel removed the ashes, and took it off the hearth; and then, after a little agitation to shake off the ashes, she wiped it with a cloth, much cleaner than I could have expected when it was laid down. It made very good and agreeable bread."

The next important advance in bread-making took place when brick bake ovens were installed in the side of the fireplace. Since the oven required the whole day to heat, the dough was mixed and placed on the hearth to rise. At bedtime when the oven would be ready, the ashes were scraped out and a bed of leaves laid inside on which the bread was baked. A long-handled wooden shovel called a "peel", was used in getting the loaves inside. By morning, the bread in all its crusty goodness was ready to be devoured by the hungry family.

It was not until the middle of the 19th century that the hearth with its bake oven was sealed off and the monstrous iron stove took its place in the kitchen.

For the wise mother who still insists that home-made bread is a necessity to her family's health and enjoyment, bread-making is an easy task as compared to that of earlier days. Today we begin with prepared yeast, either in cake or granular form, but in the old days the yeast had first to be made before thought could be given to making bread.

Making the yeast starter from hops and potatoes was a process that involved days, so care had to be taken to keep a supply always on hand. Kept tightly corked in stone jars and stored in a cool place, the yeast would stay sweet and fresh for a couple of months.

We can only imagine the regard in which these jars were held. Running out of yeast was a serious problem, particularly for those who lived in secluded areas away from a friendly neighbour who might answer a call of distress by lending some yeast from her own precious jar.

But there were other ways of getting around the problem. "Salt-Rising Bread" could be prepared in a day and the quick breads such as Bannock, Soda Bread and Corn Bread served to keep the table supplied. The distinctive flavours of these "substitutes" probably made the children look forward to the day when mother would again run out of yeast.

*The story of how Anadama Bread got its name has oft been told
— as true stories are. An old fisherman had a lazy wife. Each
day when he came home, there was nothing but cornmeal mush
— and Anna was sleeping. Finally in desperation he mixed flour
and yeast into the mush, saying over and over as he mixed, "Anna,
damn'er". And so the bread was named.*

ANADAMA BREAD

½ cup yellow cornmeal
2 cups boiling water
2 tablespoons shortening
½ cup molasses
1 teaspoon salt

1 yeast cake
½ cup lukewarm water
1 teaspoon sugar
5 cups all purpose flour

Stir the cornmeal into boiling water very slowly, stirring
continuously. Add the shortening, salt and molasses. Cook until
mixture looks like porridge. Set aside to cool. Dissolve the yeast
cake in lukewarm water with the sugar. When the cornmeal
mixture has cooled, add the dissolved yeast cake and the flour.
Knead well. Put into a greased bowl and set to rise in a warm
place until double in size. Shape into 2 loaves and place in
bread pans. Let rise again until double in bulk. Bake in a 350°
oven for 50 - 60 minutes. When baked, brush bread with warm
melted butter; turn on sides to cool.

✿ ✿ ✿ ✿ ✿ ✿

*Probably the most popular yeast bread still made today is Rolled
Oats or "Porridge" Bread. This is a good recipe for the novice to
practise on. It is a soft dough bread and is not kneaded before
it is put to rise.*

ROLLED OATS BREAD

2 cups boiling water
1 cup rolled oats
½ cup molasses
½ tablespoon salt

1 tablespoon butter
1 yeast cake
½ cup warm water
5 cups flour

Add the boiling water to the rolled oats and let stand 1 hour.
Add the molasses, salt, butter, and the yeast cake which has been
dissolved in the warm water. Lastly add the flour and mix thoroughly to distribute the yeast evenly. Let rise all day, and when
double in bulk, beat thoroughly and put into two greased bread
pans. Let rise again, then bake in a hot oven (425°) for 10 minutes. Reduce heat to 350° and bake 35 minutes more.

91

In the days of the Order of the Good Cheer, the Indians who came to the feasts at the Habitation often chose to make their meal of bread. It was a novelty to the Micmacs who did not grow wheat and therefore never knew the taste of bread before the coming of the white man.

FRENCH BREAD

1 package yeast (cake or dry)	2 teaspoons salt
1½ cups warm water	4½ cups flour
1 tablespoon sugar	

In a large bowl, dissolve the yeast in the warm water. Add sugar and salt. Add flour all at once, stirring vigorously until the dough is sticky and stiff. Set aside, free from drafts, to rise until double in bulk. Divide the dough, and working with one-half at a time, place the dough on a floured board. Roll and stretch the dough to a rectangular shape; roll into a long loaf, pinching the edges to seal, and shaping ends to a point. Place on a cookie sheet, sprinkled with cornmeal. Slit tops of loaves and let rise for 1 hour. Brush with water and bake at 425° for 10 minutes. Brush the loaves again, and bake 40 more minutes at a reduced heat (325°). Cool quickly for a crackly crust.

*   *   *   *   *   *

The following old recipe is included for interest only. We have not tested it.

SALT RISING BREAD

"Pour a pint of hot water in a two-quart pail or pitcher on one-half tablespoonful of salt; when the finger can be held in it, add one and one-third pints of flour; mix well, and leave the pitcher in a kettle of water as warm as that used in mixing. Keep it at the same temperature until the batter is nearly twice its original bulk (which will be in from five to six hours.) It may be stirred once or twice during the rising. Add to this a sponge made of one quart of hot water, two and a half quarts of flour — adding as much more as may be necessary to make a soft dough; mix well and leave in a warm place to rise. When light, mould into loaves, kneading them as soft as possible; lay in buttered tins. When light again, prick and bake."

In England, sometime in the 18th century, a young girl peddled hot buns through the streets of Bath. So popular were her wares, that a baker with a foresight for making money bought out her little business, named the buns after the girl, and Sally Lunns became a tradition. In Nova Scotia Sally Lunns are made as often in loaf form as they are in individual rolls.

SALLY LUNNS

1 cup lukewarm milk	1 teaspoon salt
1 yeast cake	3 eggs, well beaten
½ cup soft butter	3½ - 4 cups flour
¼ cup sugar	

Dissolve the yeast in the lukewarm milk. Stir in the butter, sugar and salt. Add the beaten eggs. Gradually add the flour, beating after each addition so the dough will be perfectly smooth. Cover and let rise until double in size — about 1½ hours. Spoon into a greased 10" tube pan or fill greased muffin tins ⅔ full. Let rise about 1 hour. Bake 50 to 60 minutes at 350° for large pan, and about 10 minutes in a 400° oven for muffin tins. Just before baking, sprinkle batter with sugar.

✿　✿　✿　✿　✿　✿

The favourite accompaniment to the Saturday night supper of baked beans, was brown bread. Some preferred it baked while others thought the only way was to steam it.

STEAMED BROWN BREAD

½ cup all purpose flour	½ teaspoon salt
½ cup cornmeal	½ cup molasses
½ cup whole wheat flour	1 cup sour milk
1 teaspoon baking soda	

Into a bowl sift together the flour, cornmeal, whole wheat flour, soda and salt. Add the molasses and sour milk. Stir until well mixed. Pour into a 1 - 1½ quart greased mould. Steam 2½ - 3 hours.

Before the Confederation Period, Cinnamon Bread was made in the following way: "On baking-day when the dough is light and cracked all over the surface, take out a piece weighing about 2 pounds. Melt one-fourth pound of butter in a half pint of warm milk and add this with three well-beaten eggs, to the dough. Add also a saltspoonful of soda dissolved in a little water and make the dough into a round loaf. Let it stand again until light; make deep cuts all over and fill these with a cinnamon paste, closing the dough with thumb and finger to prevent the paste running out when hot. To make the paste, work a cup of brown sugar with two heaping teaspoonfuls of cinnamon to a stiff paste, with as much butter as necessary to make the paste." Later Cinnamon Bread came to be a favourite "quick bread". The following recipe was given to us by a lady in her 80's. It was her mother's recipe.

CINNAMON LOAF

¼ cup butter	1 teaspoon baking powder
1 cup sugar	1 teaspoon baking soda
2 eggs	½ teaspoon salt
1 teaspoon vanilla	1 cup sour milk
2 cups flour	

Cream together the butter and sugar. Add the eggs and vanilla and blend well. Sift together the flour, baking powder, soda and salt and add alternately with the sour milk. Pour half of the batter in a greased loaf pan and sprinkle with half of the following mixture: 3 tablespoons brown sugar and 1 tablespoon cinnamon. Add the remaining batter and top with the rest of the cinnamon mixture. Swirl a knife through the batter to distribute the cinnamon mixture. Bake in a 350° - 375° oven for 45 minutes, or until done.

ა ა ა ა ა ა

FRIED BREAD or FANIKANEEKINS

Raised dough was used in other ways when bread supplies ran out, a favourite substitute in this case being Fried Bread, or as the Germans called it, Fanikaneekins. A piece of raised dough was rolled to ⅛ of an inch thickness, cut into squares or diamonds and set to rise for 10-15 minutes. The pieces were then fried in deep fat until well puffed and delicately brown. Served with maple syrup, this was a delicious treat.

A "spider" is a black iron frying pan that earlier had legs for use on the hearth. The legs are no longer necessary, but the spider continues to be a popular utensil whether used in the oven or on top of the stove.

SPIDER CORN BREAD

2 eggs
¼ cup sugar
2 cups sweet milk
1 cup sour milk
1 teaspoon baking soda

1 teaspoon salt
1 ⅔ cups granulated cornmeal
⅓ cup flour
2 tablespoons butter

Beat the eggs and sugar together. Dissolve the soda in the sour milk and add to the egg mixture, together with ONE cup of the sweet milk. Add the salt, cornmeal and flour. Place a spider on the range and melt the butter in it. Tilt the spider so the butter can "rup up" on the sides all around. Pour in the corn bread mixture, add the other cup of sweet milk, but do not stir in. Bake in a moderate oven (350°) for 20-30 minutes. When done, there should be a streak of custard through the bread.

❅ ❅ ❅ ❅ ❅ ❅

"Maple sugar is one of the greatest delicacies known to man, and the maple sugar of Mapleton, N.S., owing to the peculiar ore-bearing soil of the Cobequid Mountains on which the maple trees grow, is said to be unequalled by any other sweeteners in the world." — Clara Dennis, "More About Nova Scotia."

MAPLE JOHNNY CAKE

1⅓ cups all purpose flour
⅔ cup cornmeal
3 teaspoons baking powder
¾ teaspoon salt

⅔ cup milk
⅓ cup maple syrup
¼ cup shortening, melted
2 eggs, beaten

Into a bowl, sift together the flour, cornmeal, baking powder and salt. Combine the milk, maple syrup, melted shortening and beaten eggs and add to the dry ingredients. Mix well. Bake in an 8" x 8" greased pan for 20-25 minutes in a 425° oven. Serve hot.

In pioneer days the women made their linen and underclothing from flax grown in their own fields. An interesting account of a Flax-Breaking Party was recorded by Helen Creighton in <u>"Folklore of Lunenburg County, Nova Scotia."</u>

"When the flax was all pulled out we found a sunny place on the side of the hill and spread it out nice and thin and left it there for 3 weeks for the sun and rain to ripen. Then we would gather it up in a big bundle and put it on the threshing floor. A beam was put across the floor, and a comb made of wood with teeth about a foot long would take the seed out. When the seed was out we would bundle it again and let it stand for a few days in the bundles. The seed would be gathered up to dry and sieve. You could sell it or save it for planting, or make flax-seed poultice with cornmeal.

"Then we had a flax-breaking party. We had a place walled up on three sides, and a wooden grate above. We spread out the bundles and each one would take a bundle to the fire and heat it. The fireplace was about four feet high. Eight or ten women would work hard with two men to tend the fires. After it was heated it was put in the flax break and all the stubble had to be worked out of it. After the breaking was over, baskets of flax were taken to the barn again. Then they had a hetchel, about 2 feet by 1 foot, made of one hardwood plank about 1 inch thick, and another one screwed on that and pointed very sharp. Those were screwed fast to a little bench. We would sit on a stool and take handfuls of flax and strip it through, and the tow was taken out. The flax was fine like hair. The tow would be rolled in a bunch and used for the coarser things like straw sacks for beds. The fine flax would be spun in the winter evenings.

"They would carry their flax breaks with them as farm after farm was serviced through the bee. The last of the flax was thrown on the fire for good luck. Flax was woven in checkers, bird's eye, or big checks. Everybody wove their own linen, and the women wore "shimmies" to their ankles. The linen was grey at first, but was bleached with hardwood ashes and lye or put on the snow banks in the sun."

*Barley Bread is even today a great favourite among the Lunen-
burg Germans. In the old days it was made entirely of barley
flour and mixed like a cake, with a spoon.*

BARLEY BREAD

5 cups white flour	1 tablespoon salt
3 cups barley flour	½ yeast cake
2 heaping tablespoons	1 cup warm water
brown sugar	Small piece of butter

Combine the flours, brown sugar and salt. Add the yeast
cake which has been dissolved in the warm water. Mix to a soft
dough, adding more water if needed. Let rise until light, then
pour into 2 greased loaf pans. Let rise again until the dough
reaches the height of the pans. Bake in a 350° oven for 45 minutes, or until the bread leaves the sides of the pans. Brush tops
with melted butter.

* * * * * *

*Plump raisins were the "plums" in the loaf which formed part of
the fare at the Flax-Breaking Bee of old.*

OLD FASHIONED PLUM LOAF

1½ cups boiling water	Flour
1 cup mashed potatoes	2 teaspoons salt
2 cups brown sugar	1 teaspoon baking soda
2 yeast cakes	1 teaspoon nutmeg
2 cups milk, scalded	1 teaspoon cinnamon
½ cup shortening	1 pound raisins

Combine the boiling water, mashed potatoes and ONE cup of
brown sugar. Let cool. Dissolve the yeast cakes and add to the
potato mixture. Add the scalded milk, shortening and last cup
of brown sugar. Add sufficient flour to make a sponge and let
rise for 30 minutes. Add the salt, soda, nutmeg and cinnamon,
raisins, and enough flour to make dough of a good consistency
for kneading. Knead and let rise until double in bulk. Put into
pans and let rise until double again. Bake 1 hour in 350°
oven.

Soda Bread is to the Irish what Bannock is to the Scots. It was first cooked on a griddle. Sometimes the dough was placed in a Dutch Oven, the lid covered with hot embers, and the resulting loaf was nicely browned all over.

IRISH SODA BREAD

2 cups flour
1½ teaspoons baking powder
½ teaspoon baking soda
½ teaspoon salt
1 tablespoon sugar

6 tablespoons butter
½ cup light, seeded raisins
1 tablespoon caraway seeds
¾ cup sour milk

Measure and sift together the flour, baking powder, soda, salt and sugar. Cut in the butter with two knives or a pastry blender until the mixture has the consistency of cornmeal. Stir in the raisins and caraway seeds. Add the sour milk while stirring quickly with a fork. Turn dough onto a floured board and knead lightly for a moment. Shape into a round loaf about ¾" thick and place in a well-greased 8" layer cake pan. With a floured knife, make a lengthwise and crosswise mark on the dough in the form of a cross. Bake in a 350° - 375° oven for 30 - 40 minutes, or until done to a golden brown.

❀ ❀ ❀ ❀ ❀ ❀

Scottish lassies believed the eating of bannocks added beauty to the skin and sweetness to the temper. No wonder bannocks were so popular with our Scottish ancestors!

BANNOCK

3 cups flour
1 teaspoon salt
2 tablespoons baking powder

1 tablespoon sugar
2 tablespoons lard
3 cups cold water

Mix the flour, salt, baking powder, sugar and lard. Stir in enough cold water to make a thick batter that will pour. Combine quickly until smooth and pour at once into a greased baking pan. Fill the pan to half-full. Bake in a 400° oven for 35 - 45 minutes. Serve with butter and honey or a wild berry jam.

Note: Bannock will not dry up or become mouldy and will keep longer than yeast bread.

Scottish Oat Bread is more like a hard biscuit with no sweetening added. It was a great favourite of the Scots who used to bake them on a toast rack over the fire.

SCOTTISH OAT BREAD

4 cups standard oatmeal (not rolled oats)
¾ teaspoon baking soda
Pinch of salt

2 tablespoons butter
2 tablespoons shortening
Milk

In a mixing bowl, combine the oatmeal, soda and salt. Rub in butter and shortening. Add very slowly enough milk to make a fairly soft, but dry dough. Roll quite thin, about ¼", on a lightly floured board. Cut in squares or strips and brown lightly in a 375° - 400° oven. Delicious simply served with butter. "Extra special" served with cheese or cold cuts.

* * * * * *

Could it be, as we have seen written by an American cook, that "All good carrots when they die, go to Canada"? Certainly in Nova Scotia carrots are recognized as a nutritious vegetable, and through the years have made their appearance in puddings, pies, cookies, jams and even bread.

CARROT BREAD

1 cup shredded carrots
1 cup seedless raisins
4 teaspoons butter
1½ cups white sugar
1 teaspoon nutmeg
1 teaspoon cloves

1 teaspoon cinnamon
1½ cups water
2 cups all purpose flour
1 teaspoon baking powder
1 teaspoon baking soda
1 teaspoon salt

Mix together in a saucepan, the carrots, raisins, butter, sugar, spices and water. Bring to the boil and cook for 5 minutes; cool. Add the flour, baking powder, soda and salt. Combine thoroughly. Bake in a greased loaf pan for 1 hour in a 350° oven.

Graham flour was originally intended to be a cure for alcoholism. There is little doubt that it did not accomplish its purpose, but we wonder how many recipes using graham flour were originated by desperate wives of early alcoholics!

NUT BREAD

2 cups white flour	1 cup broken walnuts
1 cup graham flour	1 egg, beaten
1 cup sugar	1 cup milk
5 teaspoons baking powder	2 tablespoons melted shortening
1 teaspoon salt	

In a bowl, combine the flour, sugar, baking powder and salt. Add the nuts. Add the beaten egg, milk and shortening to the dry ingredients. Beat the mixture thoroughly. Turn into a greased loaf pan, cover and let stand for 20 minutes. Bake in a 325° oven for 45 - 50 minutes. Let stand in pan for 20 minutes and cut when completely cooled.

❋ ❋ ❋ ❋ ❋ ❋

The spicy aroma of bread baking in the oven provides a second good reason to try this old-fashioned Apple Bread. The first, is of course its delicious flavour!

APPLE BREAD

1 cup chopped apples (packed)	1 egg, beaten
½ cup chopped dates	2 cups all purpose flour
¼ cup chopped nuts	1 teaspoon baking soda
½ cup butter	½ teaspoon salt
1 cup sugar	½ teaspoon cinnamon
	½ cup sour milk

Prepare the apples, dates and nuts. Cream together the butter and sugar and beat until light and fluffy. Add the well-beaten egg and blend until smooth. Stir in the fruit. Sift together the dry ingredients and add alternately with the sour milk. Place in a greased loaf pan and let stand 10 minutes. Bake in a 325° - 350° oven until done, about an hour or less. Leave in pan for 24 hours before slicing.

SCONES, BUNS AND DOUGHNUTS

In early times bannocks and scones were the main source of bread for the Scottish settlers. Baked on the "girdle", the difference between the two is simply that the bannock is a large round cake and scones (pronounced to rhyme with "on") are formed by cutting the bannock into quarters or "farls" before baking.

Said to be born with a rolling-pin under her arm, there was no one who could make scones quite like a Scotswoman. She seemed to know by instinct the lightness with which the dough should be handled and light-handling is still the true secret of good scone-making. Superstition crept into her methods of cooking, for she believed that in kneading bannock or mixing dough, a clockwise motion must be used. It was considered unlucky to stir in the opposite direction.

Even today, it is best to follow her example and mix on a board rather than in a bowl. Using a wooden spoon, the flour should be tossed in from the sides to mix with the liquid that has been poured into a well in the middle.

Nowadays, both scones and bannocks are more often baked in the oven, but try to tell that to the Scots who cling to the old methods! If there is a wee bi' o' the bloo' o' Scotland in your veins, you may wish to use a griddle for your scone-making. In that case, we suggest that you never use grease on the griddle, but sprinkle it lightly with flour. Afterwards it should be cleaned by rubbing with coarse salt. Washing with soap and water "ta's the guid ou' o' it". Of course, we need hardly add that nothing else should ever be cooked on the scone griddle.

A woman's cooking prowess has long been measured by her ability to turn out light and fluffy biscuits. A good biscuit mix was one in which our great-grandmothers said you could "grease your elbow". This meant using lots of shortening and mixing it with the hands, which was the usual method for mixing or creaming, rather than with a fork or spoon.

The well known food consultant of New York City, Helen McCully, is a native born Nova Scotian. In a letter to us she reminisced about the delicious biscuits her mother's cook, Susan, used to make.

> *"Our relatives, the Fawcetts, were always running over to Amherst and as soon as Susan saw them coming up the drive-way, she'd put a batch of biscuits in the oven for tea. By the time they'd taken off their wraps, the biscuits would be done, piping hot layers of butter with a little flour thrown in as a binder. She probably made a cool million in her lifetime."*

The origin of the doughnut has long been the centre of controversy, with even the Indians staking their claim on its discovery. An Indian arrow piercing the centre of a Pilgrim's cake was said to have made the hole in the first doughnut. But since so many of our foods were discovered "by accident", we prefer the story that a sea-cook one day found his fried cakes to be soggy in the middle. In order to save them he simply cut out the sogginess. Strange that all of the controversy seems to lie in the discovery of the hole, rather than the delicious goodness that surrounds it! But whatever its origin, the doughnut has long been a very popular sweet and many varieties were derived through the years.

Every country home had a stone crock in which a constant supply was kept and no church supper, barn raising or work bee was complete without heaping piles of golden, tooth-teasing doughnuts.

The following recipe was given to us by a Scot in Pictou County. He still insists scones should be made on the griddle — and remember — handle lightly.

GRIDDLE SCONES

3 cups flour	¼ teaspoon salt
2 teaspoons cream of tartar	½ cup butter
1 teaspoon baking powder	⅓ to ½ cup milk

Sift together the flour, cream of tartar, baking powder and salt. Cut in the butter. Add just enough milk to make the dough stiff enough to handle. Roll out to ½" thickness on a floured board and cut into rounds about 8" across. Cut each round into four. Bake on a hot griddle, turning over until both sides are lightly browned.

❋ ❋ ❋ ❋ ❋ ❋

SULTANA SCONES

3 cups all purpose flour	½ cup white sugar
1 teaspoon cream of tartar	1 egg, beaten
½ teaspoon baking soda	½ cup milk
1 teaspoon salt	½ cup white sultanas
1 cup shortening or lard	

Combine flour, cream of tartar, soda and salt in a mixing bowl. Cut the lard in with two knives. Add the sugar, beaten egg and milk. Stir in the raisins and mix well. Roll out to ½" thickness and cut in 2" rounds or triangles. Bake in a 350° oven about 20 minutes or until golden brown.

PLAIN WHITE ROLLS

1½ cups milk
⅓ cup butter
2 teaspoons salt
⅓ cup sugar
1 yeast cake

½ cup lukewarm water
1 teaspoon sugar
1 egg, beaten
5½ - 6 cups flour

Scald the milk, butter, salt and ⅓ cup of sugar. Let cool to lukewarm. Add 1 yeast cake which has been dissolved in the lukewarm water along with the teaspoon of sugar. Add the beaten egg. Add 3 cups of the flour, beating until smooth. Add remaining flour. Toss on board to knead lightly until smooth. Cover with a tea towel and let rise until double in bulk. Toss on board again and form into rolls. Place close together in lightly greased pans to give soft sides; apart for crusty sides. Let rise, covered, until double in size. Bake in a 375° oven about 20-25 minutes, depending on how the rolls are placed in the pan. Brush tops lightly with butter after baking.

✿ ✿ ✿ ✿ ✿ ✿

CINNAMON BUNS

2 cups milk
½ cup sugar
6 tablespoons butter
1 yeast cake
¼ cup lukewarm water
2 eggs

4 cups flour
3 teaspoons cinnamon
1 teaspoon nutmeg
¼ teaspoon salt
1 cup raisins

Scald the milk and add the sugar and butter. Let cool to lukewarm and add the yeast cake, which has been dissolved in the lukewarm water. Add one egg and beat thoroughly. Add 3 cups of the flour in which the cinnamon, nutmeg and salt have been sifted. Stir in the raisins. Add the second egg and remaining cup of flour, or enough to make the dough manageable to handle. Knead; then set aside in a warm place to rise. Knead once more and let rise again. Shape into buns and bake in a 350° oven for 30-35 minutes.

Hot Cross Buns are steeped in history and tradition, having first appeared in ancient Egypt and Greece. In 14th century England, they were peddled through the streets to the old jingle "One a penny, two a penny, Hot Cross Buns". Tradition has it that if two people share a hot cross bun, they will know true fellowship. Since hot cross buns were thought to have magical powers, sailors used to wear them around their necks as a protection against disease or shipwreck.

HOT CROSS BUNS

1 cup milk	3 - 3½ cups all purpose flour
¼ cup butter	½ teaspoon cinnamon
¼ cup sugar	1 egg
1 teaspoon salt	¼ cup seeded raisins, cut small
1 yeast cake	(or currants)
¼ cup lukewarm water	

Scald the milk and add the butter, sugar and salt. Cool to lukewarm. Add the yeast cake which has been softened in the lukewarm water for 5 minutes. Add 1½ cups of the flour, and the cinnamon. Beat thoroughly. Add the egg and beat well again. Stir in the raisins. Add enough more flour, about 2 cups, to make dough just firm enough to handle and not stick to the fingers. Toss on a lightly floured board and knead to smoothness. Shape into buns or large biscuits, and place in pan one inch apart. Cover with a cloth and let rise to double in size. Brush the tops with a beaten egg and bake in a 375° - 400° oven for 15 to 20 minutes, depending on the size. Ice with a cross of frosting while warm.

*   *   *   *   *   *

Our artist, Morna Anderson, gave us her mother's recipe for these buns. Being an extremely busy woman, Mrs. Anderson finds Lazy Buns "very handy". The recipe is more than 75 years old.

LAZY BUNS

4 tablespoons butter	¾ cup milk
4 teaspoons baking powder	2 cups flour

Mix together and drop from a teaspoon on a baking sheet. Bake in a quick oven for 20 minutes.

The following two recipes are common to the Southern United States and may at first, seem out of place here. The recipes were probably brought to Nova Scotia by the United Empire Loyalists who came, bringing their Negro slaves and their cooking heritage, from the Carolinas and Virginia. A great deal of beating or kneading is necessary for these Beaten Biscuits, and they might now appear impractical to make in this servant-less age.

BEATEN BISCUITS
(Hard Biscuits)

3 cups flour
½ cup lard

½ teaspoon baking soda
1 teaspoon salt

Melt lard, soda and salt in hot water. Add to flour, and add enough cold water to make a dough that will knead well. Knead a great deal. Leave overnight on baking board with a towel turned over the mixture. Knead again in the morning. Cut in uniform pieces and shape into mounds with finger and thumb. Make a depression in the centre. Prick with a fork. Bake in a moderate oven until done.

✿ ✿ ✿ ✿ ✿ ✿

SPOON BREAD

1 cup cornmeal
2 cups milk
1 teaspoon salt
1 teaspoon baking powder

2 tablespoons melted shortening
1 cup milk
3 well-beaten egg yolks
3 stiffly-beaten egg whites

Cook cornmeal and 2 cups milk until it is the consistency of mush. Remove from heat; add salt, baking powder, shortening and 1 cup milk. Add egg yolks and fold in egg whites. Bake in a greased 2-quart baking dish in a moderate oven (325°) for 1 hour. Spoon into warm dishes; top with butter. Serves 6. Delicious with ham.

Before the advent of baking powder, the leavening agent used was a combination of cream of tartar and baking soda. Out of the past comes this recipe for Old-Fashioned Biscuits.

CREAM OF TARTAR BISCUITS

2 cups flour
2 teaspoons cream of tartar
1 teaspoon baking soda
1 teaspoon salt

4 tablespoons butter
  (or shortening)
¾ - 1 cup milk

Sift together the flour, cream of tartar, soda and salt. Cut in, or work in with the fingers, the butter. Add the milk all at once and stir quickly to blend, using as few motions as possible. Toss on a lightly floured board; cut with a floured biscuit cutter and mold into shape with the hands (using tender loving care!) Bake in a 425° - 450° oven for 12 to 15 minutes.

✳ ✳ ✳ ✳ ✳ ✳

When you make these biscuits you will open a tin of baking powder and take out the required amount. How convenient! Oft-times our foremothers made their own baking powder from a combination of ground rice, soda and tartaric acid.

TEA BISCUITS

2 cups flour
4 teaspoons baking powder
1 teaspoon salt

½ cup shortening
⅔ cup milk

Sift together the flour, baking powder and salt. With a pastry blender or two knives, cut in the shortening quickly and lightly until the mixture resembles coarse crumbs. Stir in the milk quickly with a fork, and mix just until the dough follows the fork around the bowl. Turn out on a lightly floured board, handling gently, and knead quickly 8 or 10 times. Pat the dough to ½" thickness and cut with a 2" cutter, using a straight, not twisting, motion. Place on an ungreased baking sheet, setting them apart for crusty biscuits or close together, sides touching, for soft biscuits. Bake in a 450° oven for 12 to 15 minutes. Makes 18 biscuits.

The excellence of potato biscuits depends very greatly upon the softness of the dough, light handling and quick baking. If properly made, they will be found extremely good. Ask any Irishman!

IRISH POTATO BISCUITS

6 or 8 potatoes, mashed
1 cup milk
1 teaspoon melted butter

½ cup flour (approximately)
Salt to taste

Boil and mash the potatoes. While warm, lay on a floured board and run the rolling pin over and over them until they are free from lumps. Turn into a bowl, add the milk and butter and mix well. Add salt and just enough flour to make a soft dough. Return to the board; roll out quickly and lightly into a thin sheet. Cut into rounds. Bake in a quick oven. Butter each cake as they are done, laying one on top of the other in a pile. Eat before they fall.

✿ ✿ ✿ ✿ ✿ ✿

It has been said that no one can make popovers (or Yorkshire pudding) like a Yorkshirewoman, but many delicious popovers have accompanied roast beef to the Nova Scotia dinner table. One of the secrets in making them is a hot oven, since steam is required to make the popovers "pop".

POPOVERS

Beef drippings
2 eggs
1½ cups flour

½ teaspoon salt
1 cup milk

Heat the beef drippings and pour ½ teaspoon in each muffin pan. Keep warm in the oven. Beat the eggs with a rotary beater and gradually add the flour and salt. Add the milk slowly and beat vigorously for 3 to 4 minutes. Pour into heated muffin pans and bake in a 450° - 475° oven for 15 to 20 minutes. Puncture each popover to allow the steam to escape. Serve immediately with roast beef.

From the days when muffs were worn, comes the word "muffin". "Little Muffs" were served hot to warm the fingers and appease the appetite.

CORNMEAL MUFFINS
(or Johnny Cake)

1 cup all purpose flour	½ cup cornmeal
2½ teaspoons baking powder	1 egg yolk
⅓ teaspoon salt	¼ cup molasses or honey
¼ cup sugar	¾ cup cold milk
¼ cup butter	1 egg white, beaten not too stiff

Sift together the flour, cornmeal, baking powder, salt and sugar. Cut in the butter until the mixture is of a fine texture. Add the egg yolk and molasses, blending thoroughly. Add the milk and use as few motions as possible to mix. Fold in the beaten egg white. Fill greased muffin pans not more than ⅔ full, as the mixture rises considerably. Bake at 375° - 400° for 15 to 20 minutes.

If desired, the mixture may be baked in a square, shallow pan in a 350° oven for 20 to 25 minutes. Cut in squares and serve warm with honey or maple syrup.

❊ ❊ ❊ ❊ ❊ ❊

OATMEAL MUFFINS

1 cup flour	1 cup rolled oats
3 teaspoons baking powder	½ cup chopped dates (or raisins)
½ teaspoon salt	1 beaten egg
¼ cup sugar	1 cup milk
3 tablespoons shortening	

Sift together the flour, baking powder, salt and sugar. Cut in the shortening until the mixture resembles cornmeal. Add the rolled oats and dates, blending thoroughly. Add the beaten egg and milk, stirring lightly. Fill greased muffin pans ⅔ full. Bake in a 425° oven for 15 to 25 minutes, depending on the size of the muffins.

Yield: 8 large or 16 small muffins.

The Micmacs of Nova Scotia made a blueberry "biscuit". They boiled large quantities of blueberries for 3 to 4 hours, compressed them into disc-shaped cakes, and dried them in the sun. Then they were stored in birch-bark boxes as part of the winter's provisions.

BLUEBERRY MUFFINS

1 egg	2 teaspoons baking powder
½ cup milk	½ teaspoon salt
¼ cup shortening, melted	½ cup sugar
1½ cups flour	1 cup blueberries

In a mixing bowl, beat the egg lightly. Stir in the milk and melted shortening. Sift together the flour, baking powder, salt and sugar and add to the egg mixture, stirring just enough to moisten the flour. The batter will be lumpy, so do not over-mix. Fold in the blueberries. Fill greased muffin pans ⅔ full and bake for 20 to 25 minutes in a 400° oven.

❀ ❀ ❀ ❀ ❀ ❀

In the Fall of the year, early communities buzzed with the activities of preparing apples for winter storage. After the fruit was pared, cored and quartered, it was strung on lengths of thread and hung in the kitchen to dry. The Germans called these slices of dried apples "Aeplsnits", but as far as can be determined, the procedure was followed in most colonial homes, regardless of nationality.

APPLE MUFFINS

2 cups flour	2 tablespoons melted butter
4 teaspoons baking powder	1 egg, beaten
3 tablespoons sugar	1 cup milk
½ teaspoon salt	1 cup small diced apple
2 teaspoons cinnamon and brown sugar	

Sift dry ingredients together 3 times. Add combined liquids; then add apples. Fill greased muffin pans ⅔ full and sprinkle with cinnamon and sugar mixture. Bake in a hot oven (400°) for 20 to 25 minutes.

DOUGHNUTS

3 eggs   3½ cups flour
1 cup sugar   4 teaspoons baking powder
2½ tablespoons melted butter   1½ teaspoons salt
1 cup milk   ¾ teaspoon nutmeg

Beat the eggs until foamy. Add the sugar and mix well. Add the melted butter and milk, stirring in quickly. Sift together the flour, baking powder, salt and nutmeg and combine quickly with the batter. Save ½ cup of the flour for rolling. The softer the dough the more delicate the texture, so mix a trifle softer than can be handled. Refrigerate for 2 hours, covered, so the dough will roll out much easier. Roll out on floured board to ⅜" thickness and cut. Let stand while the fat is heating. Drop into the hot fat (375°) and turn over as soon as they come to the top, which should be almost immediately. Towards the end of cooking, about 2½ minutes, turn over again. Drain on absorbent paper. Cool slightly and sugar. Store in a tin but do not cover until absolutely cooled.

* * * * * *

SOUR CREAM DOUGHNUTS

2 eggs   1 teaspoon cream of tartar
¾ cup sugar   1 teaspoon baking soda
¾ cup sour cream   1 teaspoon salt
¼ cup sour milk   ¼ teaspoon cinnamon
½ teaspoon vanilla   ⅛ teaspoon nutmeg
3 cups all purpose flour   ⅛ teaspoon ginger

Beat the eggs and add the sugar. Sift together the flour, cream of tartar, soda, salt and spices and add alternately with the sour cream, sour milk and vanilla. Leave batter in the refrigerator for 2 hours, covered. Roll out on lightly floured board to ⅜" thickness and fry in hot fat (375°) for about 2½ minutes, or until nicely browned. These doughnuts may be dropped from a spoon as soon as blended. For dropped doughnuts, lower the temperature of fat to 325°-345° (too hot a fat will not cook the inside), and cook 3 to 5 minutes.

In Lunenburg County, raised doughnuts were called Fasnaks. The name derived from the custom of making them on Shrove Tuesday, the German word for which is Fasnakdei.

YEAST or RAISED DOUGHNUTS

1 yeast cake (or package)	½ cup butter
¼ cup lukewarm water	½ cup sugar
1 teaspoon sugar	1 cup mashed potato
2 cups milk	3 eggs, well beaten
¾ teaspoon salt	6½ cups flour (approximately)

Dissolve the yeast and 1 teaspoon sugar in the lukewarm water. Scald the milk and add the salt and butter. Cool to lukewarm and add the yeast mixture. Add the ½ cup sugar to the mashed potato, mixing well, then add to the yeast mixture. Add the well-beaten eggs and about 6 cups of flour, saving ½ cup flour to use for rolling. Put the soft dough to rise until double, about 3 to 4 hours or a little less depending on the warmth of the room. Put on a board and roll to ½ inch thickness. Cut as for doughnuts, handling as little as possible. Let rise one hour. Cook in deep fat until golden brown, turning as desired. Remove to absorbent paper on a cake rack. If desired, dip the doughnuts in icing on one side.

Icing: 1½ cups icing sugar
        2 tablespoons butter
        ½ teaspoon vanilla
        Hot water, enough to make mixture of proper
            consistency to dip and glaze.

Yield: 4 dozen.

PIES

The Saturday baking, a ritual in all country homes, always included the making of several pies. Pies were an everyday dessert, topping off almost every meal including often enough, the Sunday morning breakfast. Blanc Mange or Snow Puddings were considered more presentable for company meals, and so the pie took a back seat on those occasions. Today, we are more apt to look on this in reverse, but with fruits and berries so plentiful and the "makins" for pastry always at hand, it is perhaps easy to understand how this dessert was held as "common fare".

An entire book could be written on the many varieties of pies that played a part in satisfying the sweet tooth of our ancestors. Fruit and berry pies were made in season; pumpkin and squash pies were popular in the fall after the crops had been harvested; and during the winter months, lemon, custard, and dried fruit pies kept the table amply supplied. Since many of these recipes are still in constant use and can be found in almost any cook book, we have chosen to include here the recipes that have become rare and unfortunately, in some cases almost extinct. It will be interesting to note the ingenuity

113

displayed by our great-grandmothers in finding unique ways of filling the pie crusts when fruits and berries were out of season.

Today's pie making is much easier than it was for our ancestors who did not have the advantage of regulated heat in their ovens. But they found ways of overcoming this. One rule that guided them was "If you can hold your hand in the heated oven while you count to twenty" the oven was the right temperature for baking pastry. Of course, this was only a guide and many women, some of whom could stand more heat than others, had to develop by trial and error their own standards of oven regulation.

The next problem they faced was to keep the oven at the proper temperature, for if it was allowed to cool down during the baking, the under crust would be "heavy and clammy and the upper crust fall in."

Pastry was judged by various standards — from a "very good puff paste" to a "medium puff paste" to "common paste for family use" and many of the baking tips used long ago are all but forgotten today. In some homes, it was unthinkable that even a meat pie should be adorned with anything but the finest puff pastry, made with lots of homemade butter, but there were many who considered lard to be the best shortening for a tender crust.

The best pastry was made in the "cold room" where not only the ingredients but the board, the rolling-pin, and even the hands, were cold enough to ensure that the shortening would not soften until it was popped into the oven, resulting in the desired flakiness that was the measure of good pastry. Sometimes a little baking powder was added to make the crust lighter; or sugar, to improve the colour; lemon juice to season slightly; the white of egg to improve the texture; or the yolk of egg to give it a golden hue, or gloss the outside surfaces. And we are reminded by several cooks whose reputations have long been established in their own kitchens and communities, that "It's a poor crust that will not grease its own plate."

Our recipe for making pie crust is not an old one, but we chose to include it because of its simplicity and the fact that, as the name implies, it never fails. For those who do not make pies only because they are timid about making the pastry, this recipe should reassure them. It makes enough for at least four double-crusted pies and can be kept in the refrigerator for a week. Don't overlook however, the advantage of today's freezer when making yesterday's pies, for even in the old days pies were baked in quantity during the winter months and were placed in the cold room to freeze. They would be thawed as required and baked.

NEVER-FAIL PIE CRUST
(Enough for 4 double-crusted pies)

5 full cups flour
1 tablespoon salt
1 tablespoon sugar

1 pound all-vegetable
  shortening
1 large egg

Sift dry ingredients into a large mixing bowl. Cut in the shortening. Break egg into a 2-cup measuring cup and beat with a fork. Add water to the level of the 1-cup mark. Beat again with fork. Make a well in the centre of the flour mixture and pour in the liquid, mixing lightly with fork and tossing flour in from the sides until all is moistened. Knead. Wrap air tight and keep in the refrigerator until required.

✿ ✿ ✿ ✿ ✿ ✿

The story is told of William MacDonald who planted six apple trees on his little piece of Nova Scotian ground. The Indians secretly watched the little trees grow and finally, when the first fruit appeared, they picked and ate the apples which were still in a very green state. They never touched them again, but it was a matter of curiosity to the Indians that the MacDonalds did not suffer the agonies that the fruit from the same trees had earlier brought upon them.

SLICED APPLE PIE

6 medium-sized tart apples
1 cup sugar
¼ teaspoon grated nutmeg

1 teaspoon lemon juice
2-3 tablespoons butter

Pare apples and slice thin. Place in a pie plate which has been lined with unbaked pastry, sprinkling sugar mixed with nutmeg between the layers. Sprinkle with lemon juice and dot with butter. Wet the edge of the crust with cold water and place on the top crust; seal and flute the edges. Cut slits in the top crust. Bake at 450° for 10 minutes; reduce temperature to 375° and continue baking until nicely browned and apples are tender — about 45 minutes longer.

For more than 100 years in England, mince pies were the centre of theological discussion and Puritanical clergymen preached to their flocks to abstain from this unholy fare. We are happy to say that by the time the English settlers arrived in Nova Scotia, the mince pie had been cleansed of all sin and was able to take a place of honour on the pie shelf. This is a delightfully different tasting mincemeat that has been handed down in one family for generations.

OLD FASHIONED MINCEMEAT

4 pounds lean beef
  (preferably round steak)
2 pounds fat pork
10 pounds cooking apples
  (peeled and cored)
2 pounds sultana raisins
2 pounds currants
3 packages mixed peel

3 cups granulated sugar
1 pint molasses
1½ teaspoons ground cloves
1 teaspoon allspice
1 teaspoon cassia
1 teaspoon ground nutmeg
1 teaspoon salt

Boil beef and pork thoroughly. While meat is boiling, prepare fruit and put through food chopper. When meat is boiled and partly cooled, put it through food chopper. Combine meat and fruit and mix thoroughly. Add sugar, molasses, spices, nutmeg and salt and mix thoroughly. Store in tightly covered sterilized bottles. Will keep indefinitely. When ready to use: Add ½ cup of water for every 2 cups mincemeat.
Note: If desired, ½ cup of dark rum or brandy may be added during final mixing, before bottling.

✿ ✿ ✿ ✿ ✿ ✿

Long ago, the following recipe was made all over Nova Scotia and might be placed in the "mock mincemeat" category.

HOMESPUN PIE

3 cups grated raw potatoes
2 cups grated raw apples
2 cups raisins
½ cup molasses
½ cup vinegar
3 tablespoons butter

2 cups brown sugar
½ cup mixed peel
1½ teaspoons salt
2 teaspoons cinnamon
2 teaspoons nutmeg
3 cups hot water

Combine ingredients and simmer slowly until thick, being careful not to burn. Seal hot for future use. Yield: Enough for 4 nine-inch pies.

A Scottish friend gave us this recipe for Green Tomato Mince-meat. It is very old, and is delicious and economical — especially if you grow your own tomatoes.

GREEN TOMATO MINCEMEAT

4 quarts (5 pounds) green
   tomatoes
2 pounds brown sugar
1 pound raisins
1 pound currants
½ pound mixed peel
¼ cup vinegar

½ cup butter
1 teaspoon cinnamon
1 teaspoon cloves
1 teaspoon mace
1 teaspoon nutmeg
1 teaspoon salt

Chop tomatoes and drain. Cover with cold water and bring to the boil; scald for 30 minutes. Drain. Add brown sugar, raisins, currants, mixed peel, vinegar and butter. Stir well and boil until thick (at least 2 hours or more). When cold add the spices. Keep in glass jars, sealed with wax.

Note: 1 quart green tomatoes weighs approximately 1¼ pounds. 7 pounds tomatoes and 6½ pounds sugar and fruit yields 5 large (32 ounce) jars of mincemeat.

⁂ ⁂ ⁂ ⁂ ⁂ ⁂

Nova Scotia sailing vessels brought molasses from the West Indies and in 1874, a gallon could be purchased for fifty cents.

MOLASSES PIE

1½ cups molasses
2 eggs, beaten
½ cup bread crumbs

¼ teaspoon nutmeg
¼ teaspoon cinnamon

Heat molasses. Remove from stove and add beaten eggs, bread crumbs and spices. Pour into unbaked pie shell. Make lattice work pastry and place on top. Cook until firm and pastry is done, in a 350° oven.

SUGAR MAKIN' TIME

It's April and again I turn a page in memory's book,
And walk again the mapled hills and hear a noisy brook,
In Cumberland the miracle of spring is more sublime
Than anywhere in other lands — it's sugar makin' time.

Fondly I eye the amber glow of candy on the snow,
No mortal mind can e'er concoct or man's wisdom bestow
A gift so rare to palate's bliss — God holds the recipe,
He wrote it just inside the bark of each tall maple tree.

MAPLE SUGAR PIE

2 cups milk	½ cup flour
2 egg yolks	½ teaspoon salt
¾ cup maple sugar (packed)	1 tablespoon butter

Put milk in the top of a double boiler and when hot add the beaten egg yolks to which has been added a little of the hot milk. Mix together the maple sugar and flour and add gradually to the hot milk. Remove from heat and add salt and butter. Cool. Pour into a baked pie crust and chill. Serve with whipped cream.

❀　❀　❀　❀　❀　❀

A couple of visiting Englishmen to the Middleton area stopped to watch a young girl as she collected the maple sap from the little wooden buckets. She was somewhat flabbergasted when one of the men remarked, "So this is where you Canadians get your apple juice."

MAPLE SYRUP PIE

1 cup maple syrup	2 tablespoons flour
½ cup water	2 tablespoons butter
2 egg yolks (save whites for meringue)	

Cook the above ingredients in the top of a double boiler. Pour into a baked pastry shell. Cover with a meringue made of the 2 egg whites and 4 tablespoons of sugar. Brown lightly in a moderate oven for 10 minutes.

A variation of the Maple Sugar and Maple Syrup pies was Back-woods Pie — another very old recipe.

BACKWOODS PIE

1 cup brown sugar	Butter the size of an egg
1 cup syrup (preferably maple)	3 eggs, separated
½ cup sweet milk	Nutmeg to taste

Combine ingredients and mix well together. Lastly add the 3 egg whites which have been well beaten. Pour into unbaked pie crust and bake in a 350° oven until firm.

✿ ✿ ✿ ✿ ✿ ✿

Every farm housewife made her own butter and with large quan-tities of buttermilk to use up, this came to be a popular recipe.

BUTTERMILK PIE

1 cup white sugar	1 tablespoon butter
2 tablespoons flour	2 cups fresh buttermilk
Pinch of salt	½ teaspoon lemon extract
2 egg yolks	

Combine sugar, flour and salt in the top of a double boiler. Add beaten egg yolks, butter and buttermilk. Cook until thick. Remove from heat and cool. Flavour with lemon extract. Pour into a baked pie shell. Cover with meringue. Bake until deli-cately brown in a 325° oven for 10 minutes. Note: Fresh butter-milk may be substituted by using 1 cup sour buttermilk and 1 cup sweet milk.

When there was no buttermilk, when the maple sugar and syrup were gone, and there was nothing else available, there was always Vinegar Pie.

VINEGAR PIE

1½ tablespoons flour
¾ cup sugar
2 tablespoons vinegar
½ teaspoon salt
1 tablespoon butter

Yolks of 2 eggs
¼ cup milk
1 cup boiling water
1 teaspoon lemon extract

Mix flour and sugar. Add vinegar, salt, butter and beaten egg yolks. Beat all together until creamy. Add milk and water and cook in a double boiler until mixture thickens. Flavour with lemon. Pour into a baked pie shell and cover with meringue, made with 2 egg whites and 4 tablespoons sugar. Place in a moderate oven until lightly browned.

✿ ✿ ✿ ✿ ✿ ✿

Our ancestors recognized the health-giving properties of raisins. Often they were given as a treat to children in place of the "forbidden" candy.

RAISIN CREAM PIE

1 cup seeded raisins
1 cup water
2 cups milk
2 egg yolks

¾ cup sugar
5 tablespoons flour
Pinch of salt
½ teaspoon lemon extract

Boil raisins in water for 5 minutes, then set aside. Heat milk in the top of a double boiler. In a bowl, mix together egg yolks and sugar, stirring until sugar is well dissolved. Add flour and salt. Combine egg mixture with hot milk and cook until thickened. Blend in the lemon extract and add raisins. Cool. Pour into a 9" baked pie shell, top with meringue and bake in a 325° oven for 15 minutes.

The "Pie Social" was a popular entertainment in rural areas. Each lady would bake her favourite pie and carefully pack it in a basket to share with the gentleman who "won" her with the highest bid. Sometimes envelopes with the lady's name sealed inside, were decorated in unique ways to entice the men to bid high as they were auctioned off. It was a matter of pride among the women-folk to be able to claim the highest bid of the evening. However, never let it be said that secrets were always kept, for the unmarried girls made sure that the "right" boy would recognize her envelope. And why not? It became the privilege of the "winner" to escort his lady home. The following four recipes are all pies which were popular at the Pie Social.

COCONUT CREAM PIE

1½ cups milk, scalded	¼ teaspoon salt
4 tablespoons flour	1 tablespoon butter
⅓ cup milk	½ teaspoon vanilla
2 egg yolks	1 cup coconut
½ cup sugar	

Scald milk and put in the top of a double boiler. Mix flour and ⅓ cup milk to a smooth paste and stir into scalded milk. Stir constantly until thickened. Cover and let cook about 10 minutes. Mix egg yolks with sugar and salt; add to hot mixture and cook 2 minutes longer. Add butter, vanilla and coconut. Remove from heat and cool. Pour into a baked 9" pie shell. Top with meringue and bake in a 325° oven for 15 minutes.

* * * * * *

CHOCOLATE PIE

2 tablespoons cocoa	1 cup milk, heated
2 tablespoons flour	1 teaspoon butter
1 cup sugar	½ teaspoon vanilla
2 egg yolks	

Mix together cocoa, flour and sugar in the top of a double boiler. Add egg yolks and milk. Cook until thick. Lastly add butter and vanilla. Cool. Pour into an 8" baked pie shell and top with meringue. Brown lightly in a 325° oven for 15 minutes.

LEMON MERINGUE PIE

6 tablespoons cornstarch
1 cup sugar
¼ teaspoon salt
2 cups boiling water

3 egg yolks
2 tablespoons butter
2 teaspoons grated lemon rind
5 tablespoons lemon juice

Combine cornstarch, ½ cup sugar and salt in the top of a double boiler. Gradually add the boiling water. Cook until thickened, stirring constantly. Combine beaten egg yolks and ½ cup sugar in a bowl. Stir a little of hot mixture into eggs. Blend with hot mixture in double boiler and cook 2 minutes longer, stirring constantly. Remove from heat and stir in butter, rind, and lemon juice. Cool. Pour into a cooked pie shell. Top with meringue and bake in a 325° oven for 15 — 20 minutes or until meringue is golden.

Note: Cool at room temperature to prevent honey drops on top.
Weeping: Water under meringue is caused by over-baking or poor blending of sugar.

✿ ✿ ✿ ✿ ✿ ✿

BUTTERSCOTCH PIE

¾ cup brown sugar
¼ cup white sugar
⅓ cup flour
2 cups scalded milk

⅛ teaspoon salt
3 egg yolks, beaten
1½ tablespoons butter
1 teaspoon vanilla

In the top of a double boiler, combine sugars and flour. Add scalded milk gradually, stirring constantly to a smooth mixture. Add salt and cook for about 15 minutes, stirring occasionally, till thickened. Pour part of the hot mixture onto the beaten egg yolks, stirring quickly. Pour back into double boiler, mix well, and cook not more than 3 minutes, stirring almost constantly. Add butter and stir until melted. Cool. Add vanilla. Pour into a 9" baked pie shell. Cover with meringue. Bake at 325° until very lightly browned.

DESSERTS

Possibly the most neglected course of today's meals is the dessert. A dish of commercial ice cream, canned fruit or pudding made from a mix too often serve in this department to casually top off the meal, be it lunch, dinner or supper.

Not so in great-grandmother's day, for she took the utmost care in preparing her desserts and seldom allowed a single one to reign **alone** on her table. Besides the pies, cakes and cookies, which appeared at every meal, there was always at least one more choice to be made.

Marvellous puddings, dumplings and shortcakes were among the favoured family desserts; while the lighter custards, snows, fools and whips were served with much pride when "company came callin' ".

Yet, the work involved in turning out some of these desserts was much more tedious for our ancestors. This was particularly true of recipes calling for gelatine. We have good reason to be ever grateful to an American named Charles E. Knox. Around the end of the 19th century, this man, while watching his wife laboriously preparing calf's foot jelly, hit upon an idea of packaging powdered gelatine. As an indication of the time-saver he created, we ask you to read the recipe for Calf's Foot Jelly, given at the end of this chapter. This recipe belonged to Lady Wentworth, wife of the Governor of Nova Scotia during the period 1792-1808.

The making of Blanc Mange is another good example. Today we prepare this cornstarch pudding in less than half an hour, but consider the procedure of yesteryear. The 19th century cook would add one quart of calf's foot jelly to the whites of four well-beaten eggs and set it over the fire until it boiled. Then it would be poured into a jelly bag and strained several times until it became clear. Almonds were then beaten to a paste with a little rose water and added to the jelly with a little cream. It was then returned to the fire and heated to the boiling point, after which it was stirred until almost cold and finally poured into moulds.

Who today would be willing to prepare the Blanc Mange of old for dinner every Sunday?

Old time puddings were boiled, steamed or baked, and were not always intended as the dessert, but often preceded the main course. All kinds of berries and fruits were used in the batter and the puddings were served up with a variety of delicious sauces.

Sailor's Duff is a pudding that was served on sailing vessels, usually as the Sunday dessert. It is quite like a gingerbread though it is steamed rather than baked.

Batter puddings usually take half an hour to bake, and were therefore often referred to as Half-Hour Puddings. A pudding of this type was served at political dinners in Halifax and according to the Party sponsoring, it was called either "Tory Pudding with Liberal Sauce" or vice versa.

Dumplings were also boiled and steamed, but people nowadays usually prefer them baked. Most popular of all were Apple Dumplings which were said to be "remarkably wholesome and strengthening to a weak stomach".

A type of dumpling that has long been popular in Nova Scotia is called "Grunt". The odd name is said to have come from the noises made by the fruit as it stewed in the pot. Blueberry Grunt is the best known, but strawberries, raspberries, rhubarb and apples were also used. In many homes Grunts were not considered to be desserts but were dished up in large portions as the main course.

Cobblers and shortcakes were other means of using up the abundance of fruits and berries. Cobblers were baked in the oven after the top was covered with drop dumplings. Shortcakes were made basically of a rich biscuit dough — never the sponge cake that is so often served as shortcake today.

We are fortunate that Plum Pudding came down to us through the centuries to add its glorious touch to the Christmas dinner. It almost didn't survive the Puritanical ragings that claimed it to be a sinful food. Only the delightful superstitions remain — "If you eat plum pudding on each of the 12 days between Christmas and Ephiphany and make a wish on the first bite, you will have good luck in the coming year."

PLUM PUDDING

1 pound dates	3 cups flour
1 pound seeded raisins	2 teaspoons mixed spices
¼ pound citron	2 teaspoons salt
1 cup soft bread crumbs	1 teaspoon baking soda
½ pound suet	½ cup brown sugar
1 cup molasses	

Combine and mix with warm water. Turn batter into greased moulds. Cover with waxed paper and heavy brown paper and tie tightly. Steam for 4 hours.

٭ ٭ ٭ ٭ ٭ ٭

Carrot Pudding took the place of English Plum Pudding on the German Christmas table. The following recipe has been passed down in a Nova Scotia family for generations — and no wonder. It's delicious!

CARROT PUDDING

1 cup flour	½ teaspoon cloves
1 cup raisins, chopped	½ teaspoon cinnamon
1 cup brown sugar	½ teaspoon allspice
1 cup suet	1 cup grated carrot
1 lemon, juice and rind	1 cup grated potato
4 ounces citron	1 teaspoon baking soda
1 tablespoon salt	

Mix all together, combining the soda with the potato. Steam 3 hours.

Often the captains of sailing vessels took their wives and families with them on long voyages. They would be at sea for months on end, but they loved it. Many are the tales told by captains' daughters of the experiences they remembered while sailing to Barbados or around the Cape of Good Hope.

SAILOR'S DUFF

¼ cup butter
¼ cup brown sugar
1 egg
½ cup molasses
2 tablespoons milk
1½ cups flour

1 teaspoon baking powder
Pinch of salt
½ teaspoon baking soda
1 tablespoon boiling water
1 cup seedless raisins

Combine the ingredients, dissolving the baking soda in the boiling water. Beat well. Lastly stir in ½ cup boiling water. Pour into a well-greased mould. Cover and steam for 1½ to 2 hours.

* * * * * *

It has been recorded that in the early 17th century the Micmacs used maple sap as a means of quenching thirst. Legend says they discovered it oozing from wood they were burning in the spring of the year. After that they drained the sap from the trees and boiled it in tubs by dropping hot stones into it. A lengthy process then — but even today the sap must be boiled down a great deal in order to remove the high percentage of water.

MAPLE SYRUP DUMPLINGS

2 cups pastry flour
4 teaspoons baking powder
1 teaspoon salt
2 tablespoons butter

¾ cup milk
2 cups maple syrup
2 cups boiling water

Sift together the flour, baking powder and salt. Cut in the butter, and add the milk to make a soft dough. In a saucepan bring the maple syrup and water to the boil. Drop dumplings into the syrup, cover, and cook about 20 minutes. Serve hot.

It was Charles Lamb who said "A man cannot have a pure mind who refuses apple dumplings." In the days when cooking was done on the hearth, apple dumplings were boiled in a cloth, but the ones our own grandmothers made were wrapped in pastry and baked in the oven. A delicious and still popular dessert.

BAKED APPLE DUMPLINGS

2 cups flour
4 teaspoons baking powder
¾ teaspoon salt
4 tablespoons butter or
   shortening

⅔ cup milk
½ cup sugar
Cinnamon to taste
Apples

Sift together the flour, baking powder and salt. Cut in the butter, not too fine, and add milk, mixing to a soft dough. Turn out on a floured surface and roll in a thin oblong shape, about 12" x 16". Wipe apples and core from the blossom end, being careful not to make the hole all the way through. (Apples may be peeled if preferred.) Fill each apple with the cinnamon and sugar mixture. Cut dough in sections large enough to hold an apple, and place the apple in the centre. Dampen the edges of the dough with milk and fold so that the edges meet at a centre point. Place in a greased baking dish and make a gash in the top of each dumpling. Bake in a 400° oven until the crust is set, then reduce the heat to 375° and cook until done. Serve with cream and sugar, whipped cream or lemon sauce.

❀ ❀ ❀ ❀ ❀ ❀

GINGERBREAD

¼ cup butter
¼ cup shortening
½ cup sugar
1 egg, beaten
1 cup molasses
2½ cups sifted flour

1½ teaspoons baking soda
½ teaspoon salt
1 teaspoon ginger
1 teaspoon cinnamon
½ teaspoon cloves
1 cup hot water

Cream the butter, shortening and sugar until light and fluffy. Add the beaten egg and molasses, and mix well. Sift together the flour, baking soda, salt and spices, and add. Lastly add the hot water and beat until smooth. Bake in a greased 9" x 9" pan in a 350° oven for 35 minutes, or until done.

"Poutine" is the French word for pudding; "trou" means a hole, so we might call this favourite Acadian dessert "Pudding with a Hole". Each poutine is an individual serving and can be made larger or smaller according to the size of the pastry circles.

POUTINE A TROU

3 cups all purpose flour   ¾ cup shortening
1 teaspoon baking powder   1 tablespoon water
½ teaspoon salt

Combine the dry ingredients and cut in the shortening. Add enough water to make a dough. Roll out and make circles of any desired size. Fill each circle with the following filling:

5 cups diced apple   ¾ cup cranberries
¾ cup raisins   ¼ cup fresh fat pork, diced

Combine these ingredients and fill each circle. Bring the edges of the circle together to make a ball. Place on a bake sheet with the pinched edges underneath. Make a hole in the top of each poutine and bake in a 400° oven for 40 to 50 minutes. Serve with the following sauce, which is poured into the hole of each poutine:

Brown Sugar Sauce: 1 cup brown sugar
               ½ cup water
               ½ teaspoon vanilla

Boil the sugar and water for about 10 minutes, or until the thin syrup stage is reached. Add the vanilla.

❋ ❋ ❋ ❋ ❋ ❋

AN OLD ACADIAN DESSERT

Pour fresh milk into custard cups. Cover with a cloth, placing a knife or a stick across the top to prevent cloth from touching the milk. Leave, without moving the cups for 24 hours, or until milk is thick. A coat of cream will then cover the top. Add grated maple sugar or maple syrup and serve. It is very important not to disturb the cups while they are setting.

The New Englanders who came to Nova Scotia brought with them their favourite recipes for Indian Pudding. There is a decided knack to making this pudding and if not acquired, the results could be nothing less than a soggy mess.

BAKED INDIAN PUDDING

5 tablespoons cornmeal	¾ teaspoon cinnamon
1 quart milk, scalded	½ teaspoon ginger
2 teaspoons butter	2 eggs
1 cup molasses	1 cup cold milk
1 teaspoon salt	

Scald the milk in the top part of a double boiler. Add the cornmeal very gradually and cook for 20 minutes. Add the butter, molasses, salt, cinnamon, ginger and well-beaten eggs. Put in a buttered baking dish and pour over the cold milk, but do not stir! Bake in a 350° oven for an hour, or more if necessary. Serve hot or cold with cream.

The majority of early desserts were made from the fruits that grew wild and in abundance. A common method was to stew them and add dumplings. Most often referred to as "grunt", sometimes as "slump" or "fungy", it often constituted the entire meal. Made with apples, rhubarb, strawberries, the most popular of all was Blueberry Grunt.

BLUEBERRY GRUNT

1 quart blueberries
½ cup sugar (or more)
½ cup water

Put berries, sugar and water in a pot, cover and boil gently until there is plenty of juice.

Dumplings:

2 cups flour	1 tablespoon butter
4 teaspoons baking powder	1 tablespoon shortening
½ teaspoon salt	¼ - ½ cup milk
1 teaspoon sugar	

Sift flour, baking powder, salt and sugar into a bowl. Cut in the butter and shortening and add enough milk to make a soft biscuit dough. Drop by spoonfuls onto the hot blueberries. Cover closely and do not peek for 15 minutes. Serve hot.

ORANGE PUDDING

6 oranges   1 tablespoon cornstarch
1 cup sugar   3 eggs, separated
2 cups milk

Peel and slice oranges and place in a baking dish. Sprinkle with the sugar and set aside. Scald milk in a double boiler, add the cornstarch which has been dissolved in a little cold milk. Let cook for about 15 minutes, or until thickened. Just before removing from the stove, add the three egg yolks which have been slightly beaten. When cool, pour this mixture over the oranges. Beat egg whites until stiff, add 3 tablespoons sugar and a little vanilla. Spoon over cooled pudding. Place in a 325° oven for 15 to 20 minutes or until meringue is delicately browned.

✿ ✿ ✿ ✿ ✿ ✿

STRAWBERRY SHORTCAKE

2 cups flour   ½ cup shortening
3 teaspoons baking powder   1 egg yolk
3 tablespoons sugar   6 tablespoons milk
¾ teaspoon salt

Sift together the flour, baking powder, sugar and salt. Cut in the shortening. Beat together the egg yolk and milk and lightly stir into the dry ingredients just until blended. On a lightly floured board, pat or roll the dough to ¼" thickness. Bake as one, or as individuals in a 425° oven for 10-12 minutes on an ungreased baking sheet, brushing the tops lightly with milk.

✿ ✿ ✿ ✿ ✿ ✿

BAKED APPLES

Wash and core 6 apples. Place them in a baking dish and fill each centre with a mixture made of ¼ cup sugar and 1 teaspoon cinnamon. Add six tablespoons of water around the apples. Cook in a hot oven until tender, basting frequently, for 20 to 30 minutes. Serve with cream.

Until not too many years ago, rhubarb was used in a spring tonic and given to every member of the household whether he was sick or not. The following recipe is a considerably more pleasant way of serving rhubarb.

RHUBARB COBBLER

½ cup sugar   4 cups rhubarb pieces
½ teaspoon salt   1 cup water
2 tablespoons cornstarch

Mix together the sugar, salt and cornstarch. Add the rhubarb and water and pour into a greased 9" x 9" pan. Place in a 425° oven and bring to the boil. Top with the following batter:

2 cups flour   3 tablespoons sugar
½ teaspoon salt   ¼ cup shortening
3 teaspoons baking powder   1 cup milk (approximately)

Combine flour, salt, baking powder and 2 tablespoons of the sugar. Cut in the shortening until the consistency of cornmeal. Add milk and mix to make a drop batter. Drop by tablespoons on the hot fruit mixture and sprinkle with the remaining tablespoon of sugar. Bake another 20 minutes. Serves 9.

❋ ❋ ❋ ❋ ❋ ❋

Apple Crisp served warm and with lots of thick cream is a delicious and easy-to-prepare dessert. We think it is even better when made with the top quality apples from the Annapolis Valley.

APPLE CRISP or LEVI'S PIE

4 - 6 medium-sized apples   ½ cup flour
¾ cup rolled oats   1 teaspoon cinnamon
¾ cup brown sugar   ½ cup butter

Pare apples and slice thin. Arrange slices in a greased baking dish. Combine dry ingredients and mix well. Cut in the butter. Sprinkle this mixture over the apples. Bake in a moderate oven, 350° for 35 - 40 minutes. Serve warm with whipped cream.

Almost every old cook book has a recipe for Queen of Puddings. Once we noted it was called Gypsy Pudding and were reminded of the days when gypsies roamed through Nova Scotia, telling fortunes and causing fearful apprehension among the children.

"GYPSY" PUDDING
or
QUEEN OF PUDDINGS

1 cup fine bread crumbs	¼ teaspoon salt
2 cups milk, scalded	Currant jelly or jam
2 egg yolks	2 egg whites
½ cup sugar	

Scald the milk and put the bread crumbs in it to soak. Beat the egg yolks with ¼ cup of sugar and salt, then combine with the milk and crumb mixture. Pour into a greased baking dish and set in a pan of hot water. Bake for approximately 1 hour, or until firm, in a 350° oven. Beat the egg whites until stiff, adding the remaining ¼ cup of sugar. Spread a thick layer of jelly or jam on the pudding and top with the meringue. Bake to a delicate brown, about 10 minutes. This pudding may be served hot or cold.

✿ ✿ ✿ ✿ ✿ ✿

Stale ends of bread were never tossed out by our frugal ancestors. We have to admit there was more to it than thriftiness — for bread pudding makes a very nice dessert.

BREAD CUSTARD

½ cup brown sugar	2 eggs
4 slices bread	2 cups milk
⅛ teaspoon salt	1 teaspoon vanilla

Put the brown sugar in the top of a double boiler. Place the well-buttered bread slices on top of the sugar. In a separate bowl, beat the eggs. Add milk, salt and vanilla. Pour this custard over the bread, but do not stir. Steam for 1½ hours and serve hot or cold.

HALF HOUR PUDDING

1 tablespoon shortening	½ teaspoon salt
½ cup sugar	½ cup milk
1 cup flour	½ to 1 cup raisins
1½ teaspoons baking powder	½ teaspoon vanilla

Cream shortening and mix in order given, alternating milk with the sifted dry ingredients. Put in a greased baking dish and pour over it the following sauce:

⅔ cup brown sugar	1 teaspoon vanilla
1½ cups boiling water	OR ¼ teaspoon nutmeg
¾ tablespoon butter	

Bake in a moderate oven (350°) for 30 minutes.

* * * * * *

Everybody we talked to seemed to remember Cottage Pudding as a popular dessert of their childhood. But there was a difference of opinion as to the sauce that accompanied it. As many thought this pudding should be served with a chocolate sauce as did those who preferred lemon. We'll include a recipe for both at the end of this chapter, to keep all of our older friends happy.

COTTAGE PUDDING

¼ cup shortening	¼ cup milk
½ cup sugar	1 cup flour
1 egg	2 teaspoons baking powder
1 teaspoon vanilla	¼ teaspoon salt

Cream together the shortening and sugar until light. Add the egg and vanilla and mix well. Combine the flour, baking powder and salt and add alternately with the milk. Bake in a greased pan for 20 to 25 minutes in a 350° oven. Serve with Lemon or Chocolate Sauce.

Snow Pudding, sometimes called Jordon Pudding, is not to be confused with Apple Snow. The following recipe was given to us by a lady who remembers it as her favourite Sunday dessert when she was a child.

SNOW PUDDING

2 cups boiling water
¾ cup white sugar
¼ teaspoon salt
5 tablespoons cornstarch

¼ cup cold water
2 egg whites
⅓ cup lemon juice

Add sugar and salt to the boiling water. Dilute the cornstarch with cold water and combine the two mixtures. Bring to the boiling point, stirring constantly, and let boil for 5 minutes. Then add the egg whites, beaten until stiff, and lemon juice. Turn into a mould first dipped in cold water, and chill. Remove from mould and serve with custard sauce.

Note: By using 2 tablespoons of the sugar when beating egg whites, they are easier to fold in.

Custard Sauce

3 egg yolks
¼ cup sugar
⅛ teaspoon salt

2 cups scalded milk
½ teaspoon vanilla

Beat egg yolks slightly, using a fork, then add the sugar and salt. While stirring constantly, add the scalded milk. Cook in the top of a double boiler, stirring until the mixture thickens, and a coating is formed on the spoon.

✿ ✿ ✿ ✿ ✿ ✿

APPLE SNOW

6 apples
1 lemon
½ cup sugar

3 egg whites, beaten stiff
⅛ teaspoon salt

Pare and slice the apples and cook in a very small amount of water until tender. Press through a sieve and when cold, add grated rind and juice of the lemon, sugar, egg whites and salt. Serve very cold in sherbet glasses.

134

Homemade ice cream was the highlight of old-time Sunday School picnics. Everybody took a hand at turning the crank. The following recipe requires at least a 5 quart freezer and makes a full gallon of ice cream. The freezer should be packed with 1 part freezing salt to 6 parts of ice (which has been broken into small pieces to insure compact packing). More salt hastens the freezing and less retards it. Ordinary salt may be used in place of freezing salt, but this requires more turning.

VANILLA ICE CREAM

2 quarts milk	2 tablespoons flour
4 eggs, well beaten	4 cups sweet cream (cold)
2 cups sugar	4 teaspoons vanilla

Scald the milk over hot water. Add well beaten eggs, sugar and flour. Mix well and let cook for about 30 minutes, stirring occasionally. Remove from heat and chill thoroughly. Beat the mixture well with a rotary beater and add the cream and vanilla. Pour into prepared freezer and turn it for 15 to 20 minutes, until the turning becomes difficult. Remove dasher and pack the ice cream down firmly. Then re-pack the freezer with ice and freezing salt, allowing 1 part salt to 8 parts ice. Cover the freezer with an old blanket or layers of newspapers and allow to set for an hour or two. This will further harden the ice cream and ripen it.

✿　✿　✿　✿　✿　✿

SOLID SYLLABUB

1 pint heavy cream	Whites of 2 eggs
½ cup confectioners' sugar	1 cup white wine

Whip the cream until stiff and fold in half the sugar. Beat the egg whites until stiff adding the remaining sugar. Mix well together and slowly add the wine. Serve in sherbet glasses or pour over sponge cake, macaroons or lady fingers.

GOOSEBERRY FOOL

1 quart ripe gooseberries   1 cup sugar
2 cups water   1 pint heavy cream

Top and stem the gooseberries and stew in water until tender. Press through a sieve to remove the skins. Add the sugar and stir. Whip the cream and carefully fold in the gooseberry puree. Pour into a glass bowl or individual sherbet glasses and chill.

❂ ❂ ❂ ❂ ❂ ❂

MAPLE MOUSSE

1 tablespoon gelatine   1 cup maple syrup
¼ cup cold water   ½ pint heavy cream
2 eggs   ¼ cup preserved ginger,
½ cup milk   chopped

Soak the gelatine in cold water. Meanwhile, beat the eggs and put into the top of a double boiler along with the milk and maple syrup. Stir well, and cook until mixture thickens. Add gelatine mixture and stir until thoroughly dissolved. Set aside to cool. When it begins to set, whip cream until moderately stiff and combine with the first mixture. Lastly add chopped ginger. Turn into a mould which has been dipped in cold water, or use individual moulds if desired. Chill until firm. Turn out and garnish with whipped cream.

Forach is a rich dessert traditionally served in Scottish homes on Hallowe'en. Each spoonful brought excitement to the young maidens, as each secretly wished for the wedding ring to appear on her spoon.

SCOTCH FORACH

Fine oatmeal   Whipping cream   Sugar

Take the amount of cream you think you will need and whip until stiff. Slowly stir in the oatmeal, adding enough to make the cream appear like sand. Add sugar to taste. Turn into a shallow bowl and drop a wedding ring into the contents. The family and guests each take a spoon, and all eat from the same dish. The one receiving the wedding ring in his or her spoonful of forach will be the next one in the group to be married.

❀ ❀ ❀ ❀ ❀ ❀

GINGER CREAM

1 tablespoon gelatine
¼ cup cold water
1 cup milk
2 egg yolks
¼ cup sugar
Pinch of salt

3 tablespoons ginger syrup
1 teaspoon vanilla
¼ cup preserved ginger,
    thinly sliced or cut in bits
½ pint whipping cream

Soak the gelatine in cold water for 5 minutes. Scald the milk. Beat egg yolks slightly, add sugar and salt and gradually add the scalded milk. Cook over hot water, stirring constantly until thickened. Add the soaked gelatine to the hot custard mixture and stir until dissolved. Chill; add the ginger syrup, vanilla and sliced ginger, and when mixture begins to set fold in the cream which has been whipped until stiff. Turn into a mould which has been dipped in cold water and chill until firm. Turn out and garnish with whipped cream and strips of ginger. Makes 6 servings.

One of the popular "company" desserts of the long ago was Blanc Mange. It was made with milk and Irish Moss. The moss, which is still collected on the Fundy Shore, was well washed and dried in the sun. Consisting chiefly of vegetable gelatine it was considered a very nourishing food for invalids.

IRISH MOSS BLANC MANGE

⅓ cup Irish moss   ¼ teaspoon salt
4 cups milk   1½ teaspoons vanilla

Soak moss for 15 minutes in enough cold water to cover; drain. Pick over, removing any undesirable pieces. Add the moss to the milk and cook in the top of a double boiler for 30 minutes. The milk will only thicken very slightly, but if cooked too long the blanc mange will be too stiff. Add the salt and vanilla and press through a sieve. Fill individual moulds that have first been dipped in cold water. Chill. Turn onto serving plates and serve with sliced bananas, sugar and cream.

⚬   ⚬   ⚬   ⚬   ⚬   ⚬

And now, here it is — Lady Wentworth's own recipe — in her own spelling! The lack of punctuation is interesting.

HOW TO MAKE CALF'S FOOT JELLY

"Take Two Pair of Calfes feet let them be very Clean take out the large bones put them in a Large skillet with a gallon of water let it boil away to 2 Quarts if the feet is not very Tender fill up your Skillet again and when it is boil'd away strain it through a sieve let it stand till Could then take all the fatt from the Top of your Jelly put your Jelly into a Clean skillet with the Juce of 12 Lemons the Rine of 2 a pint & half of White Wine sugar and spice to your Tast then have the Whites of 12 eggs beat to a fourth (froth) stir them in the Skillet with your Jelly then let it have one boil and pour in the fourth."

SAUCES

LEMON SAUCE

¾ cup sugar
1½ tablespoons cornstarch
¼ teaspoon salt
1¾ cups water

1 teaspoon lemon rind
1 tablespoon lemon juice
1 tablespoon butter

Combine the sugar, cornstarch, salt and water. Bring to the boil and let bubble gently for about 15 minutes. Just before serving add the lemon rind and juice and butter.

❈ ❈ ❈ ❈ ❈ ❈

CHOCOLATE SAUCE

2 tablespoons cornstarch
⅔ cup white sugar
¼ teaspoon salt
4 tablespoons cocoa

1¾ cups hot water
1 tablespoon butter
1 teaspoon vanilla

Combine the cornstarch, sugar, salt and cocoa and add the hot water. Cook over low heat, almost constantly stirring until thick and smooth. Just before serving add the butter and vanilla. Serve hot or cold.

ORANGE SAUCE

1 tablespoon cornstarch
½ cup sugar
¼ teaspoon salt

1 cup orange juice
2 teaspoons grated orange rind
5 oranges, sectioned

Mix together the cornstarch, sugar and salt in a saucepan. Blend in the orange juice gradually. Add the grated orange rind. Cook over medium heat until the mixture comes to a boil, stirring constantly. Add the orange sections.

✿ ✿ ✿ ✿ ✿ ✿

BUTTERSCOTCH SAUCE

1 cup cream
1 cup corn syrup
1 cup brown sugar

1 teaspoon butter
1 teaspoon vanilla

Place ingredients in the top of a double boiler. Cook for 1 hour, stirring once in awhile. When cooked add the butter and vanilla.

✿ ✿ ✿ ✿ ✿ ✿

HARD SAUCE

⅓ cup butter
1 cup sifted icing sugar

¾ teaspoon vanilla
1 tablespoon cream

Cream together the butter, icing sugar, vanilla and cream. Chill and serve cold.

✿ ✿ ✿ ✿ ✿ ✿

MOLASSES SAUCE

2 cups molasses
1 cup butter

4 teaspoons vinegar
1 cup water

Mix ingredients in a saucepan and cook until mixture boils up. Serve hot or cold.

CAKES

Cakes did not figure prominently in the diets of the earliest settlers. The pioneers had trouble enough trying to grind the much needed flour for bread and there was little to spare for "fancy cookin'". As one old Lunenburger put it many years ago, "Now there must be cakes and pies and everything, good, where before there was barley bread."

But as grist mills began operating, flour became more readily available and an occasional Ash Cake was enjoyed. From Perkins Hearth comes this recipe for Pilgrim's Cake:

> *"Rub two spoonfuls of butter into a quart of flour and wet it to dough with cold water. Rake open a place in the hottest part of the hearth, roll out the dough into a cake an inch thick, flour it well both sides, and lay it on hot ashes, and then [cover] with with coals. When cooked, wipe off the ashes, and it will be very sweet and good."*

Many changes have occurred in cake making since that time, and the history of cakes as we now know them really began when various leavening agents were discovered and tried. These experimentations led from purified potash made from wood ashes, to fresh fallen snow, to smelling salts, to saleratus, and then to a combination of baking soda and cream of tartar.

Eggs too, in great numbers, were used with much beating to try to obtain a light cake. A recipe for a wedding cake called for 12 dozen eggs and the batter was mixed in a wash tub. Several women must have taken part in beating a cake of that size, for hours of beating were necessary before the advent of baking powder.

By the time baking powder was available in Nova Scotia the wood stove was already in general use, and the combination of these two inventions made cake baking a great deal easier. Of course, controlled heat remained a problem, and the rules that guided the housewife appear strange and uncertain to us who are used to doing nothing more than turning a dial. "If you can hold your hand and your arm in the oven while you count to 40", the oven was just right for cakes.

We were more than once disappointed in having to by-pass some quaint-sounding cake recipes because of difficulties in conversion. Sugar and flour are both refined to a far greater extent than they once were and tastes have changed with the times. It is doubtful that you would enjoy the "Courting Cake" or "Sewing Party Cake" as they appeared in old cook books.

Measurements, too, were vague. Most old-time cooks knew by instinct when to "hurle in a Good quantity of Rasins" or just how much "a few blops of molasses" meant.

One recipe that time cannot destroy was often passed on to a bride in the hope that she would make it the pattern of her new life. It is called

HAPPINESS CAKE

1 heaping portion of true love
1 heaping cup of perfect trust and confidence
1 heaping cup of tenderness (the most tender available)
1 heaping cup of good humour (a little extra won't hurt)
1 tablespoon of good spirits (the more spirited the better)

Blend with:

1 heaping cup of unselfishness
A dash of interest in all He does
Add 1 good helping of work — to avoid this would spoil
   the flavour.

Mix all ingredients with a pint of sympathy and understanding combined. Flavour with loving companionship. Bake well all your life. Frost with kisses, fond hopes and tender words. This cake keeps well and should be served often.

The story is told in Riverport of an old gent attending a wedding feast. He was helping himself time and again to the dark fruit cake. For fear of running short, the hostess decided to offer him something else. "No thank you," he said, "this brown bread's good enough for me."

DARK FRUIT CAKE

1 pound butter	2 teaspoons ground cloves
1 pound brown sugar	1½ teaspoons salt
11 eggs	2 pounds seeded raisins
1 cup strawberry jam	1 pound sultanas (or black
¾ cup apple jelly	currants)
¼ cup molasses	½ pound candied pineapple
1 teaspoon baking soda	1 pound candied cherries
½ cup heavy cream	1 pound dates
1 teaspoon almond flavouring	½ pound chopped citron
4 cups flour	½ pound mixed peel
1 teaspoon nutmeg	¼ pound broken walnuts
2 teaspoons cinnamon	Rum

Mix in order given. Add baking soda to molasses and blend until molasses froths. Save out one cup of the flour to dust the fruit. Grease pans and line the bottoms with two layers of heavy brown paper and one layer of wax paper. Use one layer of brown paper and one layer of wax paper around the sides. Bake in a 275° oven.

Small cake requires about 2½ hours
Medium cake **requires** about 3 hours
Large cake requires about 3½ - 4 hours

Test with a toothpick or straw. Note: This recipe has been halved successfully.

143

WHITE FRUIT CAKE

1 pound butter
2 cups white sugar
8 eggs
Juice of 1 lemon
Grated rind of 1 lemon
3 cups all purpose flour
2 teaspoons baking powder
1 teaspoon salt

1½ pounds white raisins
1 pound glazed red cherries
1 pound glazed green cherries
½ pound blanched almonds
½ pound cut mixed peel
½ pound cut citron
½ pound pineapple rings
1 cup flour (for dusting fruit)

Prepare and dust the fruit with 1 cup flour. Cream together the butter and sugar. Add the eggs, juice and rind of lemon. Combine the flour, baking powder and salt and add, mixing well. Add the prepared fruit. Put into tins which have been greased and lined with one layer of brown paper and one layer of waxed paper. Bake in a 300° oven, reducing heat to 275° after the first hour of baking to prevent the cake from becoming too brown. Cooking time approximately 3 hours.

SULTANA CAKE

1 cup butter
2 cups white sugar
3 eggs
1 cup warm milk
3½ cups all purpose flour
1½ teaspoons baking powder

½ teaspoon salt
1 teaspoon vanilla
1 teaspoon lemon
½ teaspoon almond flavouring
1 pound sultana raisins

Cream the butter thoroughly and gradually add the sugar. Beat in the eggs, either separately or together. Combine the baking powder and salt with the flour and add alternately with the warm milk. Add the vanilla, lemon and almond flavourings. Lastly stir in the raisins. Bake in a well-lined and lightly greased pan in a 300° - 325° oven, for approximately 1½ - 2 hours.

PORK CAKE

1 pound fat salt pork
1 cup boiling water
1 cup raisins, chopped
1 cup citron, shredded fine
2 cups sugar
1 cup molasses

½ teaspoon baking soda
4½ cups flour
1 teaspoon cinnamon
1 teaspoon cloves
½ teaspoon nutmeg
1 teaspoon lemon juice

Chop the salt pork as fine as to be almost like lard. Pour the boiling water over it. Cool. When sufficiently cooled add the sugar, and molasses in which the baking soda has been dissolved. Seed and chop the fruit and flour well with ½ cup flour. Combine with the liquid mixture. Sift together the flour and spices and stir in, making the consistency that of a fairly stiff cake batter. You may wish to add a little more flour. Add lemon juice. Bake slowly for 2 hours in a 300° oven. Serve hot with hard sauce or lemon sauce. To reheat, steam over hot water. This recipe will yield 2 loaf cakes.

* * * * * *

DRIED APPLE CAKE
or
Farmer's Fruit Cake

2 cups dried apples
2 cups molasses
1 cup butter
2 cups brown sugar
2 eggs

1 cup sour milk
4 cups flour
2 teaspoons baking soda
1 teaspoon allspice
Nutmeg to taste

Soak the apples overnight in water. In the morning, drain and simmer in the molasses for 1 hour. Add the butter just before removing from stove. When cool add the sugar, eggs which have been well-beaten, sour milk, and dry ingredients. Pour into 2 greased loaf pans and bake in a moderate oven for an hour or less, or until done.

In England, it was a tradition for children to make a Simnel Cake to present to their mothers on "Mothering Sunday". The custom was brought to Nova Scotia, but unfortunately, has not persisted. A revival of this expression of appreciation would surely be pleasantly accepted by the mothers of this generation.

SIMNEL CAKE

¾ cup butter
¾ cup sugar
4 eggs
1¾ cups flour
1 teaspoon baking powder
¾ teaspoon salt

½ teaspoon almond flavouring
2 cups sultana raisins
¼ cup seeded raisins
½ cup chopped candied peel
¼ cup flour

Cream together the butter and sugar. Add the eggs, one at a time, mixing well after each addition. Sift together the flour, baking powder and salt and stir in. Add the almond flavouring. Dust fruit with ¼ cup flour and combine with batter. Grease a 9"x9"x3" cake pan and line with double thickness of waxed paper. Put half of batter in pan and smooth over. Lay a round of almond paste on top. Pour remaining batter over paste and bake in a 325° - 350° oven for approximately 1¼ hours. When cake is cool, top with remaining almond paste and ice.

ALMOND PASTE

1 pound almonds
4 egg yolks
½ teaspoon butter

1 pound icing sugar
1 teaspoon almond flavouring

Blanch and chop almonds and mix with egg yolks and butter. Add icing sugar and flavouring. Mold with hands. "Spank" the paste flat and flatten on the cake surface which has been moistened with water. Put on 7-8 hours before the final icing.

146

When the young Prince of Wales visited Halifax in 1860, a great ball was given in his honour. The daughter of the American consul having just enjoyed a dance with His Royal Highness, offered him this invitation: "We hope you will come to the United States. Our President will be delighted to see you, Mr. Wales".

PRINCE OF WALES CAKE

Dark Layers:

½ cup butter	2 cups flour
1 cup brown sugar	1 teaspoon cloves
3 egg yolks	1 teaspoon nutmeg
1 tablespoon molasses	½ cup sour milk
1 teaspoon baking soda	1 cup raisins
1 tablespoon hot water	

Cream the butter, adding the sugar gradually. Add the egg yolks, molasses, and soda which has been dissolved in the hot water. Blend well. Combine the flour and spices and add alternately with the sour milk. Add the raisins over which some of the flour has been sifted. Bake in two 9" layer pans in a 350° oven for 20-25 minutes.

White Layers:

½ cup butter	2 teaspoons baking powder
1 cup white sugar	½ cup milk
1 cup flour	3 egg whites, stiffly beaten
½ cup cornstarch	

Cream the butter, adding the sugar gradually. Sift together the flour, cornstarch and baking powder and add alternately with the milk. Fold in beaten egg whites. Bake in two 9" layer pans in a 350° oven for 20-25 minutes.

Spread layers with jelly, jam or icing and put together, alternating the white and dark layers. Trim the edges evenly and frost with vanilla icing.

BLUEBERRY CAKE OR PUDDING

3 cups blueberries	3 eggs, separated
½ cup butter	2 cups flour
1 cup sugar	½ teaspoon nutmeg, grated

Cream together the butter and sugar. Add beaten egg yolks, then the flour, saving out a bit for flouring the berries. Fold in beaten egg whites and nutmeg. Flour berries well and stir in. Bake in a sponge or angel cake pan in a 350° oven for about an hour.

If used as a cake, no icing is necessary. If served as pudding, use the following sauce:

Brown Sauce

2 tablespoons butter	⅓ cup brown sugar
2 tablespoons flour	1 cup boiling water
¼ teaspoon salt	¼ teaspoon vanilla

Melt the butter; add flour and salt and stir until smooth. Add the sugar and brown, stirring constantly. Remove from heat and add boiling water. Bring to the boil. Add vanilla and serve hot.

* * * * * *

GRANDMOTHER'S ORANGE RAISIN CAKE

1 orange	2 eggs
½ cup sour milk	2 cups flour
1 cup raisins	1½ teaspoons baking powder
½ cup butter	½ teaspoon baking soda
1 cup white sugar	½ teaspoon salt

Squeeze orange. Add the juice to the sour milk. Put skin through a chopper with the raisins. Keep aside 2 tablespoons of fruit and peel for frosting.

Cream the butter, adding sugar gradually. Add the eggs and beat well. Sift together flour, baking powder, soda and salt and add alternately with the milk and orange juice. Fold in the raisin and orange mixture. Turn into a 9"x9" greased pan and bake in a 350° oven. Frost with a butter icing, to which the left-over fruit and peel mixture has been added.

148

MINNEHAHA CAKE

½ cup butter　　　　　　2 teaspoons cream of tartar
1½ cups sugar　　　　　　1 teaspoon baking soda
3 eggs　　　　　　　　　½ cup milk
2 cups flour

Cream the butter, gradually adding the sugar. Add slightly beaten eggs and mix well. Add cream of tartar to the flour and stir in. Beat in milk to which the baking soda has been added. Grease two 9" layer pans, line with wax paper and grease again. Pour batter into the pans and bake for 25 - 30 minutes in a 350° oven.

Fill and frost with the following:

½ cup sugar　　　　　　2 egg whites
¼ cup corn syrup　　　　1 teaspoon vanilla
2 tablespoons water　　　1 cup finely chopped raisins

Bring sugar, syrup and water to the boil. Cook until it spins a long thread. Have the egg whites beaten stiff, and very slowly pour the hot syrup into the egg whites, beating continuously until frosting holds a peak. Add raisins and vanilla.

✳　✳　✳　✳　✳　✳

DELICIOUS CAKE

Mix in the following order:

1 cup butter ...... creamed well
2 cups sugar ...... added gradually
½ cup milk & ½ cup hot water — mixed together
1 egg
1 cup flour
1 egg
1 cup flour
1 egg
1 cup flour
1½ teaspoons baking powder (in last cup of flour)
2 teaspoons almond flavouring

Bake in a greased tube pan for 1 hour in a 350° oven.

POUND CAKE

1 pound butter
1 pound sugar
1 pound flour
10 eggs, separated

Pinch of cream of tartar
½ teaspoon real lemon juice
½ teaspoon almond flavouring
2 tablespoons brandy or rum

Cream the butter thoroughly. Gradually add the sugar and continue beating until light and fluffy. Beating is very important to the fine texture of this cake. Beat the egg yolks until thick and lemon colored. Add and beat well. Add the lemon juice, almond, and brandy or rum. Add the flour in which the cream of tartar has been sifted. Beat thoroughly for 5 minutes. Fold in stiffly beaten egg whites. Turn into a well greased and lined pan and bake at 275° for 2½ hours. Cool for 15 minutes on a rack. Remove from pan; cool and store in a tight container.

Note: ¾ of the required amount of sugar may be beaten in with the egg whites.

MAPLE SYRUP CAKE

½ cup butter
1 cup sugar
2 eggs, beaten
1 cup maple syrup
½ cup hot water

2½ cups flour
2 teaspoons baking powder
⅔ teaspoon baking soda
½ teaspoon ginger

Cream the butter, gradually adding the sugar. Add the beaten eggs and maple syrup. Sift together the flour, baking powder, soda and ginger and add alternately with the hot water. Bake in a greased angel cake pan about 50 minutes in a moderate oven. Cover with maple icing and decorate with walnut halves.

SPONGE CAKE

5 eggs (separated)
¼ teaspoon salt
¼ teaspoon cream of tartar
1 cup sugar
2 tablespoons cold water

1 tablespoon lemon juice
1½ teaspoons lemon rind
1 cup plus 2 tablespoons
    cake flour (sifted 3 times)

Add salt to egg whites and beat until foamy. Add cream of tartar and continue to beat until peaks will form. Gradually add half of the sugar, beating constantly. In another bowl, beat egg yolks and water for about 5 minutes, and then gradually add the rest of the sugar. Add lemon juice and rind and beat one minute longer. Add flour all at once and stir in until just blended. Lastly, fold in the meringue mixture until every trace of white disappears. Bake in a large ungreased tube pan in a 375° oven for 35 minutes.

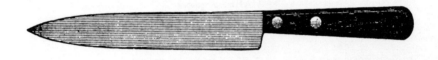

1, 2, 3, 4 CAKE

1 cup butter
2 cups sugar
3 cups flour
4 eggs, separated

1 cup milk
3 teaspoons baking powder
1 teaspoon vanilla

Sift flour and measure. Mix butter and sugar until light and creamy. Add egg yolks and beat thoroughly. Sift flour and baking powder together, and add alternately with the milk. Stir in vanilla. Lastly, fold in the beaten egg whites. Bake in a moderate oven (350°) for 1 hour. This can either be baked in a loaf pan or in layers.

OLD FASHIONED JELLY ROLL

¾ cup cake flour
¾ teaspoon baking powder
¼ teaspoon salt
4 eggs

¾ cup sugar
1 teaspoon vanilla
1 cup jelly (any flavour)

Sift and measure flour. Combine baking powder, salt, and eggs in a bowl. Place over a smaller bowl of hot water and beat with a rotary beater, adding sugar gradually until mixture becomes thick and light colored. Remove bowl from hot water. Fold in flour and vanilla. Do not beat if you prefer your jelly roll to be light. Turn into a jelly roll pan (15"x10") which has been greased and lined with waxed paper. Bake in a hot oven (400°) for 13 to 15 minutes. When cake is baked turn out on a towel, peel off waxed paper and roll tightly, towel and all. Let cool. Unroll carefully and spread with jelly. Roll again, wrap in towel and slice when ready to serve.

٭ ٭ ٭ ٭ ٭ ٭

MARBLE CAKE

White Part:

1 cup white sugar
½ cup butter
3 egg whites
½ cup milk
2 teaspoons baking powder
1 teaspoon vanilla
2½ cups flour

Dark Part:

1 cup brown sugar
½ cup butter
3 egg yolks
½ cup sour milk
½ cup molasses
1 teaspoon baking soda
1 teaspoon salt
2 teaspoons cinnamon
1 teaspoon cloves
2½ cups flour

White part: Beat egg whites until stiff. Add sugar and beat again, then add butter, milk, vanilla and baking powder which has been combined with the flour.

Dark part: Beat egg yolks. Add sugar, butter, molasses and beat well. Add milk and sifted dry ingredients. Drop by tablespoonfuls alternately in a loaf pan. Bake in a moderate oven (350°) for 1 hour.

FRENCH CREAM CAKE

3 eggs
1 cup sugar
1½ cups flour

2 teaspoons baking powder
3 tablespoons water

Beat the eggs until light and foamy. Add the sugar and mix thoroughly. Combine flour and baking powder and sift into batter. Lastly add the water. Pour batter into 2 well-greased 9" layer pans and bake for 25-30 minutes in a 350° oven. Cool.

Filling:

2 eggs
½ cup sugar
4 tablespoons flour

2 cups scalded milk
1 tablespoon butter
1 teaspoon vanilla

In the top of a double boiler beat the eggs. Add sugar and flour and mix well. Gradually add hot milk, stirring constantly, and cook until thickened and smooth. Put over boiling water and continue to cook another 10 minutes. Remove from heat and stir in butter and vanilla. Cool.

Split each layer in two, giving 4 layers. Spread the filling between the layers and dust with sifted confectioner's sugar.

✿ ✿ ✿ ✿ ✿ ✿

IRISH CHOCOLATE POTATO CAKE

1 cup butter
2 cups sugar
4 eggs
3 ounces unsweetened
  chocolate, melted
1 cup cold mashed potatoes
1 cup sour milk

2 cups flour
1 teaspoon baking powder
½ teaspoon baking soda
¼ teaspoon salt
1 teaspoon cinnamon
¼ teaspoon nutmeg

Combine the ingredients in order given. Pour into two greased and lined 9" layer pans and bake in a 350° oven for 35 minutes, or until done. Cool in pans for 10 minutes, then turn out and cool on racks. Fill and ice with chocolate butter icing. Because this cake is very moist and will keep beautifully it needs a good, rich icing that will keep well and not dry out. (See next page).

153

RICH CHOCOLATE BUTTER ICING

¼ cup butter
2 squares unsweetened chocolate, melted
3 cups icing sugar (at least)
Hot water — to make of right consistency

Beat vigorously; add 1 teaspoon vanilla.

✿ ✿ ✿ ✿ ✿ ✿

MAPLE SUGAR FROSTING

¾ cup grated maple sugar
¼ cup white sugar
¼ cup water
1 egg white, stiffly beaten

Combine the maple and white sugars with the water and bring to the boil. Boil until the syrup spins a long thread. Pour syrup gradually into the beaten egg whites, beating vigorously. Continue beating until the frosting stands in stiff peaks.

✿ ✿ ✿ ✿ ✿ ✿

MAPLE SYRUP ICING

¾ cup maple syrup
¼ cup white sugar
1 egg white

Place in a double boiler over boiling water. Beat until it forms peaks. Cook and beat another 2 minutes.

COOKIES AND LITTLE CAKES

Grandmother's cookie jar was an institution which we had previously thought to be totally North American in origin. During our research we were proven wrong on this assumption, for the English had their "biscuits" and macaroons, the Irish their cheese cakes and the Scots their wafers and "toddies". The Scoth "cukie" we saw referred to as far back as 1671, and since the Scottish equivalent to the English "bun-fight" or tea-party was called a "cooky-shine", we can hardly claim the cookie to be an American invention. Nevertheless, Grandmother's earthen cookie crock with its seemingly never-ending supply is well established in the memory of almost every adult Nova Scotian — no matter from where their ancestors came.

In Nova Scotia, the earliest cookies were baked in sheets and cut in squares or broken into pieces after baking. Later, dough was marked in grooves by way of a corrugated roller making the cutting easier and of a regulated size. After this came the wooden cookie moulds which applied patterns to the dough, thus adding a decoration that must have delighted the small fry.

The Scots had long fashioned their oatcakes into "farls" by cutting a circle around an inverted plate, after which the circle was cut into quarters. This procedure is still followed in the making of scones.

Individual cookie cutters probably came into being after our ancestors had improvised their own cutters by using the top of a tumbler or ordinary tea-cup to cut the rolled dough into rounds. The local tin-smiths or the family handy-man took it from there and used their own imagination in forming shapes of animals, hearts and stars into tin cutters, sometimes adding a handle and sometimes not.

Drop cookies were made, as in the case of the English "Rock Biscuits", when bits of the dough were put onto the pans with a fork and made to look "as rough as possible". Small amounts of dough were also molded into "the shape of a nut" and pressed down with the bottom of a tumbler or the tines of a fork, just as we still do nowadays.

Our great-grandmothers revealed their ingenuity again by utilizing whatever was available as a means of getting the cookies to the oven. Sometimes cake or roasting pans were inverted to form a make-shift cookie sheet; other times, heavy paper was greased and used for the same purpose.

Molasses and ginger cookies were the most widely made, since molasses was a common and inexpensive sweetener and spices were considered a staple in every household. White sugar, when it became available, was used in baking cakes and shortbreads only for such special occasions as a wedding, a christening, or when the minister came to call. Maple syrup and sugar were other popular sweeteners, but the early recipes calling for maple sugar are now more economically made with brown.

There are those who claim that ginger snaps can never taste as good as the ones made in the old wood-stoves of our great-grandmothers. Perhaps it is in ignorance of the earlier product that we can mark our seal of approval on those that come from today's electric range.

The amount of spices used in ginger cookies was left to the individual cook's own taste. We have noted, in equivalent amounts of cookie dough, as little as ½ teaspoonful to as much as 2 tablespoonfuls of ginger, with varying amounts of other spices such as "sinnament" and powdered cloves being used also, according to taste.

Sugar cookies were always more fun to eat when raisins were pressed on top to form "funny faces". This was a job given to a little girl as her first cooking experience — and how she loved doing it!

SUGAR COOKIES

1 cup butter
1 cup sugar
2 eggs, well beaten
Flavouring to taste

2½ cups all purpose flour
2 teaspoons cream of tartar
1 teaspoon baking soda

Cream the butter and sugar together until light and fluffy. Add the well beaten eggs and flavouring. Lastly add the dry ingredients which have been sifted together. Roll not too thin, about ¼", and sprinkle with granulated sugar. Bake 10 minutes in a **375°** oven. Using a 2" cookie cutter, this makes about 5 dozen cookies.

✿ ✿ ✿ ✿ ✿ ✿

The following recipe has been used in the homes of a Truro family for at least 100 years. Chicken fat, in place of the shortening, added flavour to the original recipe.

GINGER SNAPS

½ cup white sugar
1 cup molasses
½ cup hot, melted shortening
½ cup clear, hot tea
1 teaspoon baking soda

3½ - 4 cups all purpose flour
1 teaspoon salt
2 teaspoons ginger
½ teaspoon cloves

Put sugar and molasses into a mixing bowl. Dissolve the baking soda in the hot tea and add, together with the shortening, to sugar mixture. Let stand until lukewarm, then add the dry ingredients. Chill dough overnight, or at least 2 hours, before rolling out. This chilling improves the flavour and makes the dough easier to handle. The dough should be rolled thin (about ⅛") and more flour may be added, if necessary for easier handling. Bake in a 400° oven for 8 to 10 minutes.

157

Before cookie cutters were available, rolled-out dough was sometimes scored with a fork, first down, then across, creating a "plaid" pattern on the cookies when cut into rounds with a tumbler or tea-cup.

LONG JOHNS
(Old-Fashioned Soft Molasses Cookies)

½ cup shortening
½ cup butter
1 cup white sugar
1 cup molasses
1 egg
3 teaspoons baking soda
¾ cup boiling water

1 tablespoon vanilla (optional)
3-4 cups all purpose flour
1 teaspoon cream of tartar
1 teaspoon salt
½ teaspoon cinnamon
½ teaspoon ginger
½ teaspoon cloves

Cream together the shortening, butter and sugar until light. Blend in the molasses and egg. Dissolve the soda in boiling water and add to the mixture; add vanilla. Sift together the dry ingredients and add gradually, mixing well to make a soft dough. Cool. Roll out to ¼" thickness. A little more flour may be added, but just enough to make dough easy to handle. Bake in a 375° oven for 8 to 10 minutes.
Yield: 6 - 7 dozen.

❈ ❈ ❈ ❈ ❈ ❈

The following recipe is a delicious example of the way maple syrup was used for baking in days gone by.

MAPLE SYRUP COOKIES

1½ cups maple syrup
½ cup white sugar
½ cup shortening
1 teaspoon baking soda

1 cup rolled oats
½ teaspoon salt
2 cups all purpose flour

Heat the maple syrup, sugar and shortening to boiling point. Remove from stove and add the soda which has been dissolved in a little warm water. Let cool. When cold, add the rolled oats, salt and flour enough to roll out. Roll not too thin and cut with a cookie cutter. Bake in a 375° oven until light brown, about 8 to 10 minutes.

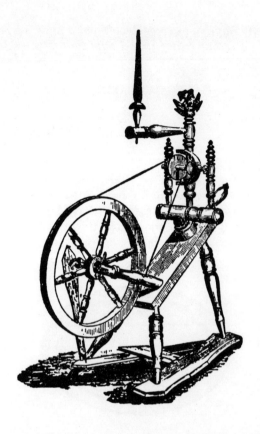

Our Scottish ancestors used "real" oatmeal and no sweetening when they made their favourite oatcakes. However, sugar did creep in, as indicated by this 75 year old recipe. Made with the nutty-flavoured oatmeal from Balmoral Mill, Colchester County, the Scots say there's nothing can beat them.

PICTOU COUNTY OATCAKES

2 cups oatmeal
1 cup flour
1 cup brown sugar
1 teaspoon salt

¾ cup shortening
¼ teaspoon baking soda
¼ cup boiling water

Combine dry ingredients and cut in shortening. Dissolve baking soda in the boiling water and add, continuing to mix with a knife. Mold with the hands and shape into a long wedge. Slice off and bake in a 400° oven for 10 minutes.

159

For those who have not as yet developed a taste for Scottish Oatcakes, here's a recipe using rolled oats that was made in Grandmother's day.

OAT CAKES

3 cups rolled oats	½ teaspoon salt
3 cups flour	2 cups shortening
1 cup sugar	½ cup cold water

Combine the rolled oats, flour, sugar and salt in a large bowl. Cut in the shortening or work it in with the hands, until the dough is manageable. Moisten with cold water. Roll, not too thin, using rolled oats on the board to prevent the dough from sticking. Cut into desired shapes, or use a knife and cut into diamonds or squares. Bake in a 350° oven for 15 minutes.
Yield: 6 - 7 dozen.

The following recipe is probably one of more recent years, but is such a favourite in Nova Scotia that it cannot be excluded.

CRISPY CRUNCH COOKIES

1 cup butter	1 teaspoon vanilla
1½ cups brown sugar	1½ cups all purpose flour
1 egg	2 teaspoons baking powder
1¼ cups rolled oats	1 teaspoon salt
1½ cups coconut	¼ teaspoon baking soda

Cream the butter and gradually add brown sugar. Add the egg and beat well. Stir in rolled oats, coconut and vanilla. Lastly add dry ingredients which have been sifted together. Form into balls the size of a walnut, place on a greased cookie sheet and flatten with a fork. Bake in a 375° oven for 10 - 12 minutes.

Hogmanay is the Scottish New Year's Eve, and the serving of shortbread to those who go visiting from house to house has long been a custom among the Scots.

HOGMANAY SHORTBREAD

3½ cups all purpose flour ½ cup fine fruit sugar
or 3 cups pastry flour 1 cup chilled, hard butter

Sift flour and sugar together and rub butter into the mixture. (The butter must be hard, because the texture depends on long working with the hands.) In about 15 minutes, the crumbs should be soft enough to be kneaded into a ball. Knead for about 5 minutes until the ball of dough is smooth. Shape into two flat, round cakes about 1" thick. Place into 9" pie plates. Pinch edges and prick all over and right through with a fork. Bake at 250° - 275° about one hour or until lightly browned. Leave in tins until completely cooled. Serve in pieces broken off from cooled cake, or cut in wedges while hot. Store in tightly covered tin in a cool, dry place.

✿　✿　✿　✿　✿　✿

Scotch Cakes are simply small shortbreads, rolled, or preferably patted, into desired thickness and cut in fancy shapes with tiny cutters. In making shortbreads never use any shortening other than butter.

SCOTCH CAKES

1 cup butter (unsalted)
4 tablespoons brown sugar
2 cups all purpose flour

Cream butter until very light. Add the brown sugar and blend together until fully dissolved. Add the flour gradually. Toss on a very lightly floured board and knead, adding only enough additional flour until the dough shows cracks as you knead it. Pat gently to ½" thickness, and cut into shapes. Place on lightly floured cookie sheet and bake in a 325° oven for 20 - 25 minutes, or until very delicately browned. Cool on racks.

161

Old-time "Rocks" were a favourite cookie for generations, though how they survived such an unappealing name is a mystery. Raisins or currants sometimes replaced the dates, and in one old recipe, the dried fruits were ignored altogether, with the walnuts being increased to 2 cups.

GRANNIE'S ROCKS

1 cup butter	1 pound chopped dates
1½ cups brown sugar	1 cup broken walnuts
3 egg yolks, beaten	1 teaspoon baking soda
½ teaspoon cloves	1 tablespoon hot water
¾ teaspoon cinnamon	2¾ cups all purpose flour
1 teaspoon salt	3 egg whites

Cream the butter and gradually add sugar. Add egg yolks and beat well. Add the remaining ingredients, dissolving the soda in the hot water, and lastly folding in the egg whites which have been beaten stiff, but not dry. Drop on a greased cookie sheet and bake in a 350° oven for 10 - 12 minutes. Do not over-bake.

❄ ❄ ❄ ❄ ❄ ❄

The Acadians and the New Englanders both lay claim to this old cookie recipe and we prefer not to take sides on that controversy.

JUMBO RAISIN COOKIES

2 cups raisins	1 teaspoon baking powder
1 cup water	1 teaspoon baking soda
1 cup shortening	2 teaspoons salt
2 cups white sugar	½ teaspoon cinnamon
3 eggs	½ teaspoon nutmeg
1 teaspoon vanilla	¼ teaspoon allspice
4 cups all purpose flour	1 cup chopped nuts (optional)

Cover raisins with water and boil 5 minutes. Cool. Cream together the shortening and sugar. Add the eggs and beat well. Add vanilla and boiled raisins with ¼ cup more water. Sift together the dry ingredients and add to the batter, a little at a time. Lastly, add the chopped nuts. Drop on a greased cookie sheet and bake in a 375° oven for 10 - 12 minutes.

The history of Eccles Cakes is older than Nova Scotia. These delicious little pastries having been made for centuries in England, were peddled through the streets during Wake Week celebrations.

ECCLES CAKES

Short pastry
½ cup chopped raisins

½ cup chopped walnuts
8 tablespoons strawberry jam

Roll pastry about ¼" thick and cut into 3" squares. Put about a tablespoon of filling on each square, and, after moistening the edges, fold the four corners to centre. Join well and turn them over, then press or roll slightly until the filling just begins to show. Make two little slits in the top, place them on a greased cookie sheet, and brush with a mixture of egg and water. Bake in a hot oven (400°) until lightly browned - about 20 minutes.

✿ ✿ ✿ ✿ ✿ ✿

The years have brought about many changes in these little cakes. Very early recipes called for puff paste and a dozen eggs. Our version comes from a recipe many years old and is still delicious, though far less expensive.

MAIDS OF HONOR

1 cup butter
2 cups flour

4 tablespoons icing sugar
Raspberry jam

Cut the butter into the flour; add sugar and knead until well blended. Line patty pans with this rich pastry. Put a half teaspoon of raspberry jam in each tart and add one teaspoon of the following mixture.

½ cup butter
½ cup white sugar
2 small eggs, well beaten

½ cup rice flour
1 teaspoon almond flavouring
Few grains of salt

Cream butter and sugar together; add the eggs, flour, flavouring and salt. Place 1 teaspoonful in each patty shell and bake in a hot oven (400°) about 12 minutes, or until a nice brown.

How these little tarts got their name remains a mystery to us. It could be that pork fat was once used as the shortening, or it might just be a reflection of the wonderful Cape Breton sense of humour.

CAPE BRETON PORK PIES

Tart Shells

1 cup butter   2 cups flour
4 tablespoons icing sugar

Cut the butter into the flour; add the sugar and knead until well blended. Press small amounts of dough into small muffin tins. Bake in a 425° oven for 10 minutes. When cool fill with the following:

Filling

2 cups chopped dates   1 cup water
1½ cups brown sugar   Lemon juice

Simmer the above ingredients until the dates are of a soft consistency. Cool; then fill the tart shells. Ice with butter icing.

* * * * * *

Always on baking day, Grandmother made sure there was enough pastry dough left over to turn out a few dozen Butter Tarts. Even today at County fairs there are special awards for the best butter tarts, and this award is vied for and coveted by the winner.

BUTTER TARTS

¼ cup butter   ½ cup seedless raisins or
1 cup brown sugar   currants
1 egg, beaten   1 tablespoon lemon juice

Pour boiling water over the raisins and let stand for 5 minutes to soften; drain. Cream the butter. Add sugar gradually and mix thoroughly until light. Add beaten egg, a little at a time, blending well after each addition. Stir in the drained raisins and lemon juice. Fill pastry-lined tart tins with a teaspoonful of the mixture and bake in a 375° oven for 15 - 20 minutes or until pastry is a golden brown.

1 lb. ¼. Butter
½ c. Rice flour
1 " White Sugar
4½ " all purpose flour

275 oven for 1 hr.

Parker jotter Pen
Parker

JAMS AND PICKLES

The preserving of fruits and vegetables was a necessary labour of love in every home. From the first sign of wild berries in the spring through to harvest time, fruits and vegetables not hardy enough to "keep" in their original form would be preserved, by one method or another, for winter use.

Wild strawberries and blueberries were often simply dried in the sun. These could later be used in cakes and pies or steeped in water to make a palatable drink. Blueberries would also be placed in wooden kegs, covered with water and allowed to ferment, providing a tasty sauce to serve up with meat or pancakes.

Fruits preserved without cooking were said to retain their original flavour much better than those that were cooked. One such method called for the paring and quartering of larger fruits, such as peaches, to be spread on large flat plates and sprinkled, pound for pound, with sugar. These were then placed before a slow fire or in a just-warm oven. After a rich preserve was formed, the fruit was placed in earthen or glass jars and covered over with brandied paper

Preserving each fruit in its season took some time, beginning with the picking. But a break in daily routine was always regarded as a time for fun, and Blueberry Picking Days were especially looked forward to by old and young alike.

165

Early in the morning, the entire family of women and children would set out with empty pails and a packed lunch. When they returned at dusk, their backs might ache but their pails were full and their spirits high. Sometimes there were exciting tales to tell since it was often necessary to build small fires to keep the bears away from the picking area.

Throughout the summer months the kitchens would intermittently hum with the activities of jam and jelly making, but in the fall there was a constant hustle as garden vegetables were brought in for pickling. Beans, beets, cauliflower, cabbage, corn, green tomatoes, onions, peppers and cucumbers — all had to be carefully prepared and stored against the long winter ahead.

The pickle barrel has now disappeared, but it was once the focus of some attention. Cucumbers were picked daily from the vine, taken to the cellar and carefully packed in barrels, according·to their size. Salt was spread over each layer, forming a brine from the extracted juice so that no addition of water was needed. A weight placed on a wooden cover which was a little smaller than the top of the barrel, kept the pickles under the brine. In this way pickles could be preserved for years, but before eating, a procedure of freshening and "greening" was necessary.

Finally the work was done and the housewife could view with pride the fruits of her labours. Now was the time for neighborly visits. An invented excuse, perhaps to borrow a cup of sugar, always ended in a guided tour through the cellar — the hostess near exploding with pride and the visitor mentally comparing her own accomplishments.

The entry to the cellar was usually outside the house. Two sloping doors had to be raised in order to gain the steps that led down to the cool darkness. Walls were lined with stones and the floor was of packed earth.

First the crocks and barrels were shown and inspected, and then the tour led past the long shelves that reached from the rafters to the floor. Here were rows and rows of neatly arranged jars, each marked according to its contents. A count of each variety was proudly given by the hostess, for prosperity was measured not by money but by the quantities of provisions stored in that personal mint — the cellar.

The method of making honey without the bee's assistance is said to date back to the 17th century. While gathering the clover, be on the look-out for the four-leafed variety. Should you find one, look well upon it but do not pick it. Some of the old folks here still believe that seeing a four-leaf clover brings good luck, but picking it brings grief.

HOMEMADE HONEY

80 blossoms white clover	10 cups sugar
40 blossoms red clover	3 cups water
5 rose petals (faintly perfumed)	½ teaspoon powdered alum

Combine the sugar, water and alum and boil for 5 minutes. Pour the syrup over the blossoms and rose petals and let stand for 20 minutes. Strain through a cheesecloth and bottle. Store in a dry place.

✿ ✿ ✿ ✿ ✿ ✿

During our childhood we were always told to eat our daily orange for its Vitamin C content. But what of our ancestors before oranges were imported into Nova Scotia? Well, there were apples, blackberries, currants and strawberries. And there were rose hips. Rose hips are the hard round berries left on the wild rose. High in natural Vitamin C, they were used in making jams, jellies and purees.

ROSE HIP JAM

2 pounds fresh rose hips	1 cup sugar (or more)
1¼ cups water	

Remove stems, seeds and blossom ends from rose hips. Wash quickly. Bring to the boil and simmer, covered, for about ½ hour or less, until tender. Strain through a sieve and weigh the pulp. Add 1 cup of sugar for every pound of pulp. Bring to the boil, stirring continuously, and boil for 10 minutes. Pour into hot jars, cool and seal.

PUMPKIN JAM

5 pounds pumpkin   1 orange, sliced thin
4 pounds sugar   Few grains of salt
3 lemons, sliced thin

Remove peel and cut pumpkin into pieces about ¼" thick and 1" to 2" long. Place in a bowl, add sugar and let stand overnight. Remove the pumpkin pieces, bring the liquid to the boil and cook until it will spin a thread. Add pumpkin, lemons, orange and salt. Cook slowly until thick and clear. Bottle. Makes about 6 pints.

✿ ✿ ✿ ✿ ✿ ✿

The following recipe is, in our opinion, worth the price of this book. Pure and simple, the addition of a few under-ripe berries adds natural pectin. Try it and spoil your family as ours have been spoiled.

STRAWBERRY JAM

2 quarts strawberries,   6 cups sugar
   hulled

Place berries in a kettle over heat. Crush as they heat. When berries boil, add sugar and cook quickly until thick, no longer than 20 minutes, stirring frequently to prevent burning. Pour into clean hot jars and seal. Makes 2 quarts.

Note: This recipe is not as good when doubled so we suggest making only 2 quarts at a time.

✿ ✿ ✿ ✿ ✿ ✿

This would seem to be the spot for another personal favourite. Don't be fooled by the canned pineapple and packaged gelatine for these were both products of the 19th century.

RHUBARB AND PINEAPPLE JAM

4 cups rhubarb, cut in ½" pieces   1 can (20 ounces) crushed
2 packages strawberry jello   pineapple, not drained
   powder   5 cups sugar

Mix rhubarb and sugar. Add pineapple. Place on high heat and bring to the boil. Reduce heat and boil for 20 minutes. Remove from stove and stir in jello powder until dissolved. Cool and bottle.

GOOSEBERRY JAM

4 cups gooseberries
5 cups sugar

1 cup hot water
1 teaspoon Epsom salts

Wash gooseberries and remove stem and blossom ends. Cook the gooseberries, sugar and hot water for 30 minutes. Add Epsom salts and cook 15 minutes longer. Remove from heat and pour into clean hot jars and seal.

Bishop Charles Inglis, who arrived in Nova Scotia in 1787, had in later years a country home near Auburn, Kings County. Here he practised husbandry and experimented with new species of apples. One of these, the Bishop Pippin, was named for him and has become deservedly famous.

APPLE JELLY

3 pounds firm, tart apples
Sugar

3 to 5 cups water

Choose any tart, juicy apple which is barely ripe for best results. Wash apples, remove stem and blossom ends; cut in quarters. Then slice the quarters, skins, cores and all, into a preserving kettle. Add cold water to barely cover. Cover kettle and bring to a boil. Reduce heat and simmer without stirring until apples are soft (about 10 to 15 minutes). Crush apples with a potato masher and cook 5 minutes longer. Turn into a jelly bag made from two thicknesses of cheesecloth, suspend over a bowl and let drip. Do not squeeze bag. Measure juice and boil for 5 minutes. Add ¾ cup sugar for every cup of juice and continue boiling until two drops run together to form sheet when dropped from the edge of a metal spoon. Skim jelly and pour into hot clean glasses. Seal and keep in a cool, dry place.

Duelling was banished in Nova Scotia by 1850, with the last military duel at Halifax proving to be quite an amusing affair. The seconds had loaded the pistols with powder and mashed cranberries. The duellists, quite prepared to see blood were, nonetheless, shocked by the ensuing results.

CRANBERRY JELLY

4 cups cranberries   1½ cups sugar
1½ cups water

    Pick over and wash berries. Bring the berries and water to the boil and boil for 20 minutes. Press through a sieve and add sugar to the juice. Boil hard for 5 minutes. Pour into jelly jars.

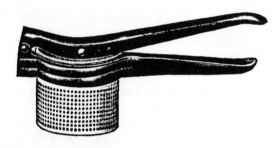

The Scots are credited with the discovery of marmalade, and their breakfast table is world renowned. Dr. Johnson once told his Boswell that no matter where he supped, he wished he could always breakfast in Scotland, so impressed was he by the wide variety and excellence of Scotch marmalade and preserves.

CITRUS MARMALADE

3 oranges   9 - 10 cups water
1 lemon   8 cups sugar
1 grapefruit

    Wash fruit and put in a saucepan, whole. Nearly cover with water. Bring to the boil and cook for 30 - 45 minutes, or until fruit is soft enough to pierce with a fork. Turn occasionally. When done, save 2 cups of the juice. Remove fruit to a platter and let cool slightly. Cut up and put through a fine chopper. To the fruit add the reserved juice and sugar. Bring to the boil and cook for 20 minutes. Bottle.

CARROT MARMALADE

6 medium carrots
3 oranges (bitter)
2 tablespoons grated lemon rind

3 tablespoons lemon juice
White sugar

Scrape and dice the carrots finely; cook, drain and dry. Grind the oranges and combine with carrots. Add the lemon rind and juice. Measure and add ⅔ cup sugar for every cup of mixture. Let stand overnight. Bring to a rapid boil and cook until clear and like marmalade. Bottle.

✻ ✻ ✻ ✻ ✻ ✻

Although a favourite spread for bread and rolls, Lemon Curd was often used to fill tart shells. It will keep for a long time if covered tightly and stored in the refrigerator.

LEMON CURD

6 eggs
3 lemons, juice and rind

2 cups sugar
½ cup butter

In the top of a double boiler, beat eggs well and add juice and rind of lemons, sugar and butter. Blend well and cook, stirring almost constantly, until it is as thick as honey. Pour into a jar and cool.

✻ ✻ ✻ ✻ ✻ ✻

Barely legible, in a fine old script, we found this recipe among the pages of an old account book.

SPICED GOOSEBERRIES

4 quarts gooseberries
8 cups brown sugar
1 pint cider vinegar

1 teaspoon nutmeg
1 teaspoon cinnamon
1 teaspoon allspice

Put all together and cook slowly for about ¾ hour. Bottle and store.

SPICED CRABAPPLES

7 pounds crabapples,
   blossom ends removed
8 cups sugar
4 cups vinegar

1 cinnamon stick
½ teaspoon root ginger
¼ cup whole cloves

Tie the spices in a bag and add to the sugar and vinegar. Bring to the boil, then add the "crabs" which have been washed and pricked in several places. Cook quietly until tender but not broken. Remove spice bag and fill hot jars with hot fruit and syrup. Seal at once.

✿ ✿ ✿ ✿ ✿ ✿

RHUBARB RELISH

1 quart rhubarb, diced
1 quart onions, finely cut
1 pint vinegar
1 pound brown sugar

1 teaspoon salt
1 teaspoon pepper
1 teaspoon whole cloves
1 teaspoon whole allspice

Cook rhubarb and onions in vinegar for about 20 minutes. Add sugar, salt, pepper and the spices which have been tied in a bag. Boil ½ hour longer. Bottle.

✿ ✿ ✿ ✿ ✿ ✿

CORN RELISH

18 large ears corn
1 medium cabbage
6 large onions
3 sweet green peppers
2 sweet red peppers

4 cups sugar
1 quart vinegar
½ cup mustard
1 tablespoon tumeric
4 tablespoons salt

Wash and cut cabbage; peel onions. Wash and cut peppers and remove seeds. Put cabbage, onions and peppers through the food chopper. Strip corn from cobs and add to other vegetables. Sprinkle with the sugar. Combine vinegar, mustard, tumeric and salt and pour over vegetables. Boil for half an hour, then bottle.

SWEET RED PEPPER RELISH

8 large, tart apples
½ cup water
12 sweet red peppers

2 lemons
4 cups white sugar

Peel, core and cut up the apples. Add the water and cook over low heat until mushy and soft. Wash, seed and chop the red peppers (or put through medium food chopper). Cover with cold water and bring to the boiling point; drain quickly and well. Return the peppers to kettle and add the lemons which have been put through a fine food chopper. Boil gently, uncovered, about 20 minutes or until the peppers are nearly tender, stirring occasionally. A very small amount of water may be added if required. Add the sugar and cooked apples; simmer together until thick, for about 15 minutes. Pour into hot jelly jars and seal.

CHOW CHOW

15 pounds green tomatoes
5 pounds onions
½ cup salt
1 quart vinegar
½ teaspoon cloves
½ teaspoon mixed spice
½ teaspoon allspice

2 teaspoons cinnamon
1 teaspoon dry mustard
3 cups sugar
Cayenne pepper (if desired)

Prepare vegetables and sprinkle with salt. Let stand overnight. In the morning, drain. To 1 cup of the vinegar add the spices, mustard and sugar. Add to the remaining vinegar and pour over vegetables. Boil for 2 hours or more. Bottle.

TEN DAY PICKLES

6 pounds small onions   1 small basket gherkins
2 cauliflower   1 cup pickling spice
                                  (in gauze bag)

Hot brine: ¾ cup salt to 1 quart water

Syrup: 1½ quarts white vinegar to 3½ cups sugar

Prepare the vegetables and pour over them the brine, making enough to cover. Repeat on the third and sixth days. On the ninth day, drain. Flush well in cold water. Make enough syrup to cover and let stand overnight. (This syrup is a bit tart, so for a sweeter pickle, add more sugar.) On the tenth day remove the spices and vegetables. Strain the syrup and heat. Place vegetables in bottles and cover with syrup.

❀ ❀ ❀ ❀ ❀

SWEET MUSTARD PICKLES

12 cucumbers (small basket)   1⅓ cups flour
1 cauliflower   6 cups sugar
3 pounds small onions   4 teaspoons tumeric
½ cup salt   4 tablespoons dry mustard
                               2 quarts vinegar

Prepare vegetables and sprinkle with salt. Let stand overnight. In the morning drain and rinse. Combine the flour, sugar, tumeric and dry mustard. Blend in the vinegar and cook, stirring constantly, until thickened. Pour over the vegetables and if necessary, add enough vinegar to cover. Simmer for ½ hour over low heat. Bottle.

PICKLED BEETS

Beets   6 cups brown sugar
3 cups water   2 tablespoons salt
6 cups vinegar

Wash beets and cook until tender. When done, peel and cut in cubes or slices. While warm, place in heated bottles and pour over them the hot liquid, to cover completely. The liquid is made by combining the water, vinegar, brown sugar and salt and bringing just to the boiling point. Do not boil.

✿ ✿ ✿ ✿ ✿ ✿

PICKLED BEANS

1 peck golden wax beans 1 cup flour
Salt   1 dessertspoonful tumeric
3 pints vinegar   1 cup mustard
2½ pounds sugar

Boil beans slowly in salted water until tender. Drain. Let vinegar and sugar come to the boil. Mix the flour, tumeric and mustard into a smooth paste with a little vinegar. Pour into the hot vinegar and boil 5 minutes. Then add beans and cook gently for 5 minutes more. Add salt to taste.

✿ ✿ ✿ ✿ ✿ ✿

FRUIT SAUCE PICKLE

15 ripe tomatoes, peeled and ½ bunch celery, chopped fine
 cut up   1 pint vinegar
3 onions, chopped fine 1¼ teaspoons salt
3 peaches, cut up   Small bag of mixed spice
3 pears, chopped fine   3 cups white sugar
3 apples, chopped fine

Prepare fruit and vegetables and simmer all together for 3 hours, or until thick. Bottle and seal.

TOMATO CATCHUP

1 peck ripe tomatoes	½ ounce ground mace
1 quart vinegar	2 tablespoons dry mustard
1 cup sugar	1 tablespoon ground cloves
2 cloves garlic	1 teaspoon ground allspice
6 tablespoons salt	1 teaspoon red pepper (cayenne)

Cover the tomatoes with water and bring to the boiling point, then drain well and run them through a sieve or press through a vegetable press. Put the pulp into a porcelain-lined pan, add all the other ingredients and simmer for six hours. Bottle and seal.

✻ ✻ ✻ ✻ ✻ ✻

MUSHROOM CATCHUP

1 peck mushrooms	2 tablespoons mustard
1 cup water	1 teaspoon cinnamon
1 pint vinegar	½ teaspoon mace
2 tablespoons salt	½ tablespoon cloves
½ teaspoon cayenne pepper	

Pick over, wash and drain the mushrooms, slice and put over the fire in a saucepan with 1 cup water. Cook until mushrooms are soft, stirring often. Press through a sieve. To the pulp add the vinegar, salt, cayenne, mustard, cinnamon, mace and cloves. Boil half an hour longer. Bottle and seal.

✻ ✻ ✻ ✻ ✻ ✻

PICKLED EGGS

12 hard-cooked eggs	½ teaspoon mustard seed
3 cups white wine vinegar	4 - 8 whole cloves
2 tablespoons sugar	4 bay leaves
1 teaspoon salt	1 or 2 chili peppers

Bring vinegar to a boil with other ingredients. Shell eggs, being careful not to break them. Put eggs in a glass jar and cover with vinegar mixture which has been allowed to cool slightly. Seal and put in refrigerator. These should stand a week to ten days before using.

BEVERAGES

It is said that Nova Scotians drink more rum per capita than any other people in North America. This is not to say that Nova Scotians imbibe more liberally, but when they do, their preference is, or long has been — rum.

Traditionally, this is understandable, when we think back to the early days of English settlement in Nova Scotia. Halifax was a garrison town and the American home of the Imperial Fleet. It has long been a tradition in the Navy that each man would receive his daily portion of grog. In those days, at least, this procedure applied also to the garrison troops. The daily grog allowance seems rather a generous one, consisting of one gill of rum to three gills of water. But if this was not enough, quantities of rum were still easily obtained since it was said to be "as cheap as water, and a sight more plentiful."

Rum was considered by the pioneers to be an essential commodity. Just as nowadays, we hear of the oldsters who slyly take a nip of brandy or glass of wine "for medicinal purposes", this was very much the case in the early days. Winters were longer and colder then, and rheumatism was the scourge of the time. How a man could weather the long winters without the warmth of rum to fortify him could hardly be imagined before the days of the Temperance Societies.

Every country store had its keg of rum, complete with spigot and mug, and usually with a dried, salted codfish hanging on the side. Portions of the fish were torn off at will and eaten as an appetizer. This strategically placed "tid-bit" certainly served its purpose in developing even greater thirsts and, naturally, the sales from the keg were increased.

Not everyone, however, drank rum. The Scots preferred their Scotch whiskey, the Irish their rye, while the gentility drank wine — port, madeira and claret being the prevailing wines for gentlemen. But it was a hard-drinking age and the proportions consumed were vast as compared to today's glass at the dinner table. It is interesting to note that the Prince of Wales and twenty friends manfully finished off 64 bottles of old Madeira at one sitting.

Nor was the drinking strictly reserved for grown-ups. At militia and troop reviews, boys were furnished with a drink known as "shrub", which was composed of rum, peppermint and aniseed. Even in the Orphan's Home at Halifax in the 1750's, spruce beer was served "as a substitute for rum" because it was "so condusive to health". Does one assume then, that rum was the beverage given to children before the health-rendering qualities of spruce beer were universally recognized?

Of course, there was milk to be had on the farms and country children were encouraged to drink buttermilk as well, since it was supposed to help the digestion. But town children in those early days did not have milk, except on very rare occasions.

Before leaving the subject of spruce beer, it may be of interest to note the claim that this beverage was invented by the New Englanders during the first seige of Louisbourg, the French fortress on Cape Breton Island. We have reason to question this, since it has been recorded in early writings that spruce beer was brewed by the Acadian French as far back as the early 17th century. We are told that the Acadians learned it from the Indians and then "improved" the recipe by adding yeast and molasses. Nevertheless, during the seige of Louisbourg spruce beer was served daily to the troops as a means of warding off scurvy.

While the townsfolk enjoyed their negus, wassails and sillibubs, the country folk had their cider and home-made wines. The methods for many of these home-brews came down through generations and were originally learned from the Indians. Teas, brewed from spruce leaves, tips of maple trees, leaves or bark of hemlock, twigs of yellow birch, winterberries and roots of sassafras, all sufficed to make the beverages of the Micmacs. These teas were largely used by the white people as remedies and therein, perhaps, lies their greatest value.

This old method for making spruce beer was recorded in Thomas H. Raddall's "Halifax, Warden of the North".

HOW TO MAKE SPRUCE BEER

"*Take 7 pounds of good spruce and boil it well till the bark peels off. Then take the spruce out and put in 3 gallons of molasses and boil the liquor again, scum it well as it boils, then take it out of the kettle and put into a cooler. When milk-warm in the cooler put a pint of yeast into it and mix well. Then put it in the barrel and let it work for 2 or 3 days, and keep filling it up as it works out. When done working, bung it up with a tent-peg in the barrel to give it vent now and then. It may be used in 2 or 3 days.*"

✿ ✿ ✿ ✿ ✿ ✿

A later version of spruce beer calls for spruce extract which simplifies the recipe considerably.

SPRUCE BEER

1½ cups sugar	1 teaspoon vanilla
1 quart boiling water	4-6 packages of dry yeast
3 quarts cold water	2-3 tablespoons spruce extract

Dissolve the sugar in the boiling water. Add the cold water and vanilla. Sprinkle the yeast over and combine until well blended. Lastly add the spruce extract. Cover and set in a warm place to ferment about 12 to 16 hours. Remove the scum and bottle. Keep in a cool place.

TO MAKE A SACK POSSET

"Beat up the yolks and whites of 15 eggs, strain them and then put ¾ pound of white sugar in a pint of Canary and mix it with the eggs in a basin. Set it over a chafing dish of coals and keep continuously stirring it until it is quite hot. Next grate some nutmeg in a quart of milk, boil it, and then pour it into the eggs and wine. While pouring, hold the hand very high and let another person keep stirring the posset, which renders it smooth and full bodied to the taste."

SODA NEGUS

"A most refreshing and elegant beverage, particularly for those who do not take punch or grog, is thus made:

Put ½ pint of port wine, with 4 lumps of sugar, 3 cloves and enough grated nutmeg to cover a shilling, into a saucepan. Warm it well, but do not suffer it to boil. Pour it into a bowl or jug, and upon the warm wine decant a bottle of soda water. You will have an effervescing and delicious negus by this means."

✻ ✻ ✻ ✻ ✻ ✻

DRINK FOR THE DOG DAYS

"A bottle of soda water poured into a large goblet in which a lemon ice has been placed, forms a deliciously cool and refreshing draught; but it should be taken with some care, and positively avoided whilst you are very hot."

180

In 1606, Champlain recorded at Port Royal: "Snow came on the 6th of October. There are 6 months of winter in this country. Our liquors all froze, cider (in casks) was handed out by the pound."

APPLE CIDER

7 pounds apples   1 gallon water
3 pounds sugar

Use fallen apples which have no rot, and have not been touched by frost. Baldwins are best, but any small apples will do. Cut up the apples and place in an earthen crock. Cover with cold water and let stand, protected with a cover of muslin, for 10 days, stirring each day. When fermentation has ceased, strain through a jelly bag. Return juice to the crock and add the sugar, stirring until sugar is dissolved. Leave for 7 days, stirring daily. Skim and pour into a wooden keg. Cork tightly. This will be ready for use in 6 months time.

✿ ✿ ✿ ✿ ✿ ✿

MULLED CIDER

2 quarts cider   1 teaspoon whole cloves
¾ cup brown sugar   1 teaspoon whole allspice
3 sticks cinnamon

Mix cider and sugar in a kettle. Add spices which have been tied in a cheesecloth bag. Boil for 10 minutes. Remove the spice bag and serve hot.

✿ ✿ ✿ ✿ ✿ ✿

MINUTE CHAMPAGNE

"If you are about to drink sharp cider, put half a teaspoonful of carbonate of soda and a dessertspoonful of finely-powdered sugar at the bottom of your glass; have the cider poured on this, and you will allow that it is a very pleasant, though humble, imitation of champagne."

181

GINGER BEER

1 ounce ginger roots	1 lemon, rind and juice
1 teaspoon cream of tartar	1 gallon boiling water
1 pound sugar	1 ounce yeast

Break the dry ginger roots and add the cream of tartar, sugar and grated lemon rind. Pour over the boiling water and stir until the sugar is dissolved. Let stand until just warm. Stir in the yeast and lemon juice. Cover and set in a warm place to ferment for 24 hours. Skim off the yeast and bottle. Let it rest for 3 days before using.

DANDELION WINE

1 gallon dandelion petals	1 orange
1 gallon boiling water	1 lemon
4 pounds sugar	1 yeast cake
	1 slice toast

Pick the petals from the dandelions, throwing away the stems and heads. Put flowers into a crock and pour over the boiling water. Cover and leave about 10 days, stirring occasionally during that period. Strain off the flowers and put liquid into a large kettle. Add sugar. Peel the orange and lemon very thinly and add peel. Remove the white skin and seeds from the fruit, cut up and add to the liquid. Boil for about 20 minutes and return to the crock. When cool, spread the yeast on a slice of toast and add. Cover and leave for 2 days. Remove to a 5 gallon cask and cork. Let it ferment for at least 2 months, then bottle.

Blueberries probably were the first familiar foodstuff found by the settlers. The type that grew in Nova Scotia was almost identical with the hurtleberries of England and Scotland.

BLUEBERRY WINE

For each quart of berries add one quart of cold water. Put in an open mouth jar or clean firkin to mash.

Every day mash and stir them well for one week, then strain through a cloth and allow 3½ pounds of sugar to each gallon of juice.

Mix well and cover lightly. Keep in a warm place to ferment. Skim every day till all the thick scum has worked off, then put in a jug. Tie a muslin over the mouth.

Let stand in a warm place to work for three weeks or until "it is done singing", then cork and let stand three or four weeks to settle. Bottle carefully.

    ✿ ✿ ✿ ✿ ✿ ✿

PORT WINE

2 pounds whole wheat	1 pound seeded raisins
1 pound currants	1 pound sultana raisins
5 pounds white sugar	4 good-sized potatoes, diced

Pour over six quarts boiling water. When cool, add 1 yeast cake dissolved in warm water. Stir every day for 20 days. Strain. Add 1 pound sugar, 10c worth isinglass, 10c worth burnt sugar. Let stand 2 days. Strain and bottle.

PARSNIP WINE

5 pounds parsnips
9 pints water
4 pounds sugar (or less)

1 piece root ginger
2 lemons or oranges

Clean and cut parsnips. Do not peel. Boil in water for 2 hours with ginger. Add water to keep up to 9 pints. Strain. Let cool a bit. Add sugar, oranges or lemons, cut up. Stir and boil again for 5 minutes. Put all in a crock or jug. When cool, add toast with yeast on top. Cover. Stir each day for 21 days. Strain and bottle.

* * * * * *

MANGLE WINE

4 pounds mangles
10 pints cold water

Peel and cut mangles in small pieces. Cover with water and boil 10 minutes or longer. Drain. Throw mangles away. Boil again with:

4 pounds white sugar
2 lemons, sliced

Boil for 10 minutes, then let cool and add yeast cake. Let stand in a crock in a warm place for 2 weeks. Bottle and leave corks loose for 2 more weeks.

RED BEET WINE

12 large beets	3 pounds white sugar
5 quarts water	A little black pepper
2 pounds raisins	1 yeast cake (spread on a piece of toast)

Boil finely-cut beets in the water until colourless and tender. Strain through cheesecloth adding enough water to still make 5 quarts. Put back on stove and add 3 pounds sugar and a little black pepper. Boil 10 minutes and strain again. Pour in a crock and when lukewarm, add raisins and toast with yeast. Let ferment 3 weeks or more. Strain again and bottle but do not force corks too tight. This makes 4 quarts and should age.

PARSLEY WINE

½ pound of parsley leaves (no stems)	½ root ginger, crushed
¼ pound raisins, pulled open	Juice and rind of 2 lemons
½ ounce yeast	Juice and rind of 2 oranges
3½ pounds sugar	1 gallon water

Wash parsley and boil for 1 hour. Keep water up to amount. Add sugar and stir until dissolved. When liquid is tepid spread 1 yeast cake on toast. Leave for 21 days. Stir twice daily with wooden spoon. Siphon.

RHUBARB WINE

5 pounds rhubarb, cut in pieces
Put 1 lemon through chopper and add to it.

Pour over this 1 gallon boiling water. Let stand 3 days. Add 4 pounds sugar and 1 yeast cake dissolved in water. Let stand 2 days and strain again. Add 20 beets isinglass. Let stand 3 months and bottle.

SEED WHEAT WINE

2 pounds seed wheat
4 potatoes, peeled and cut fine
1 pound currants
2 pounds raisins

4½ pounds sugar, browned
1 yeast cake
6 quarts water

Let stand 20 days. Strain and add isinglass and burnt sugar to make colour of port. Let stand 3 weeks. Strain and bottle. Add 1 teaspoon or more of brandy to each bottle.

❅ ❅ ❅ ❅ ❅

CORN MEAL WINE

1 pound corn meal
2 pounds brown sugar
2 pounds raisins

1 yeast cake
1 lemon, sliced thin
4 quarts cold water

Mix well and stir twice each day for 4 days. Let stand 4 weeks. Strain and bottle.

In haying time, swinging the scythe was a very thirsty task. Under a clump of evergreen bushes nearby was kept a jug of Switchel. Nothing, it is said, was so refreshing as this cooling drink.

HAYMAKER'S SWITCHEL

1 gallon water
2 cups brown sugar
1 cup molasses

1½ cups vinegar
1 teaspoon ginger

Mix all ingredients together. Pour into a jug and hang in the well to cool.

✿ ✿ ✿ ✿ ✿ ✿

RASPBERRY VINEGAR

3 pounds raspberries
1 pint cider vinegar

Sugar

Mash the berries with a wooden spoon and cover with vinegar. Let stand 24 to 36 hours, stirring frequently. Strain through a double cheesecloth and add one pound of sugar to one pint of juice. Boil for 10 minutes. Bottle.

✿ ✿ ✿ ✿ ✿ ✿

LEMONADE

½ ounce Epsom salts
2 ounces citric acid
1 ounce tartaric acid
5 pounds white sugar

3 pints boiling water
6-8 lemons, sliced
4 oranges, rind only

Combine the Epsom salts, citric acid, tartaric acid and sugar in a large saucepan. Add the boiling water and stir until dissolved. Cool. Add lemon slices and orange rind. Using the proportions of 2 ounces of this syrup to 8 ounces of water, this recipe makes about 4 quarts.

IRISH COFFEE

1 cup hot black coffee
Sugar to taste

2 ounces Irish whiskey
1 heaping tablespoon whipped
    cream

    Warm a large stemmed goblet. Put a spoon into the goblet and add hot coffee. Sweeten to taste and add Irish whiskey. Top with whipped cream. Serve at once.

✿ ✿ ✿ ✿ ✿ ✿

The dish that he'll to supper teuk
Was always Atholl Brose. — Gaelic Verse

ATHOLL BROSE

2 parts honey
1 part whiskey

6 parts cream

    Mix the honey and whiskey together in a bowl. Add the cream, stir, and ladle into wine glasses.

✿ ✿ ✿ ✿ ✿ ✿

AULD MAN'S MILK

6 eggs
1 cup sugar

1 quart new milk or thin cream
½ pint brandy, rum or whiskey

    Separate yolks and whites of eggs. Beat the egg yolks and add sugar and milk. Stir until dissolved. Add the brandy, rum or whiskey, a little at a time. Beat egg whites to a froth. Pour the liquor into a punch bowl and very gently add and mix in the egg whites. Grated nutmeg may be added to taste. Serve in punch glasses.

CANDIES

Candy was a very rare treat for the children of the early pioneers. Sugar was scarce and "dear", pennies were too precious to be squandered and sweet treats were something everyone could do without. So the children lived in anticipation of the time when the sap would run again in the maple trees — for early spring was the time for Candy on the Snow.

When the sap was collected and in the process of being boiled into maple sugar, the older folks always made sure that a little of the boiling liquid was poured on the snow where it hardened into a delicious candy. The sweet-starved youngsters pounced upon it with glee and ate their fill, fully realizing that it might be a long time before they could again enjoy the sweet taste.

As time passed, molasses candy began to be made more and more frequently until finally it became an almost weekly treat. Half the fun was in the making and taffy pulls became a much-loved pastime with the younger set.

In 1844, Mott's Chocolate Factory was established at Hazelhurst in Dartmouth, and the long sticks of chocolate that sold in the stores for a penny soon became a most popular product.

Even as late as 1876, however, there seemed to be very little money to buy candies in quantity. An old Accounts Journal of that year from a general store near Musquodoboit, noted only an occasional sale of five or ten cents worth of candy. It is highly likely that pennies passed over the counter to pay for a candy or two, and only the larger amounts appeared in the records.

By 1902, advertising was playing its role in pushing the sale of candy. In Pelton's Journal (a monthly magazine edited by two teenaged brothers in Yarmouth) there appeared this interesting advertisement:

"If you should chance to walk down street
In search of candy pure and sweet,
Just walk into Barteaux's Cash Store
And see the case right near the door.

'Tis filled with candies good to eat,
With chocolates, twenty kinds or more,
So if your friends you wish to treat,
Don't pass by Barteaux's Grocery Store.

You're sure to find there chocolates nice,
White's, Webb's, Ganong's, all of renown,
You're sure to get the lowest price,
Of candies sold in town.

Peppermint	15c lb.
Conversation Lozengers	20c lb.
Ribbon Candy	10c lb.
Good Chocolates	15c lb.
Gum Drops	15c lb.
Cream Mints	15c lb.
Webb's Chocolates	40c lb.
White's Chocolates	35c lb.
Newport Chocolates	40c lb.
Best Mixed Candy	25c lb.
Good Mixed Candy	8c lb.
Ganong's G.B. Chocolates	40c lb."

MOLASSES TAFFY

3 tablespoons butter   2 cups molasses
⅔ cup white sugar

Melt the butter in a saucepan. Tip the pan to grease the sides. Add molasses and sugar and stir until sugar is well dissolved. Bring mixture to a boil, stirring slowly all the while. Cook and test by dropping a bit of the mixture into cold water. When it becomes brittle (265°) the candy is done. Pour into a well-buttered platter to cool until it can be handled. Grease the hands and pull the taffy from hand to hand until it becomes firm and turns a golden color. Draw into a smooth band or twist into a rope. Cut into short lengths, using the kitchen scissors. Wrap pieces in waxed paper.

* * * * * *

VINEGAR CANDY

2 cups white sugar   2 tablespoons butter
½ cup vinegar

Melt the butter in a saucepan and tip the pan to grease the sides. Add the sugar and vinegar and stir until sugar is well dissolved. Cook slowly without stirring until brittle when tested in cold water (265°). Pour on buttered platter to cool. Pull and cut as for molasses taffy.

* * * * * *

VELVET KISSES

1 cup molasses   3 tablespoons vinegar
3 cups white sugar   ½ teaspoon cream of tartar
1 cup boiling water   ¼ teaspoon baking soda
½ cup melted butter   Vanilla

Put molasses, sugar, water and vinegar in a saucepan. When it comes to the boil add cream of tartar and boil until mixture becomes brittle in cold water (265°). Stir constantly during the last part of the cooking. When nearly done add soda and melted butter. Remove from stove and add flavoring. Cool and pull as for molasses taffy.

191

Since the time of Marguerite Bourgeoys, who founded the Congregation of Notre Dame and opened the first Canadian school in 1658, it has been the custom in all the houses of the Order to observe the feast of Saint Catherine of Alexandria, a virgin martyr who died on November 25, 307 A.D.

In all the boarding schools of the Sisters of the Congregation of Notre Dame, the pupils have the privilege of sharing with the Sisters this delicious molasses candy, which in French is called "La Tire" (pronounced lah teer). The custom has spread over all of French Canada and spinsters over 25 implore good Saint Catherine's aid as they make this traditional candy. St. Catherine is the patron saint of unmarried girls, especially of those over 25 years of age.

LA TIRE (Saint Catherine)

1 cup molasses	½ cup water
1 cup white sugar	1 tablespoon butter
1 cup brown sugar	1 tablespoon vinegar
½ cup corn syrup	1 teaspoon baking soda
	(no lumps)

A few drops of vanilla may be added for special flavour

Put all ingredients except soda into a deep saucepan. Boil until mixture forms a hard ball in cold water (250°). Add soda and mix well. Pour contents into a well-buttered platter. Let cool until candy can be handled. Pull with both hands until candy becomes a golden brown, or lighter shade if desired. Cut in small pieces and wrap in bits of waxed paper.

✿ ✿ ✿ ✿ ✿ ✿

EVERTON TOFFEE OR BUTTERSCOTCH

2 cups white sugar	1 cup butter
2 cups dark molasses	Grated rind of half a lemon

Boil over a slow fire until it will snap and break (hard crack - 290°). Pour, not too thick, into well-buttered pans. Cool slightly and mark in squares.

SUCRE LA CRÉME

1½ cups brown sugar
1 cup white sugar
2 cups maple syrup

1 pint whipping cream
Nuts or coconut (if desired)

Cook slowly until a soft ball forms in cold water (235°). Remove from heat and cool slightly. Beat until creamy, adding nuts or coconut just before pouring. Pour into well-buttered pan and cut in squares.

❅ ❅ ❅ ❅ ❅ ❅

MOLASSES FUDGE

1 cup brown sugar
1 cup white sugar
¼ cup butter
½ cup molasses

½ cup cream
2 squares unsweetened
   chocolate
½ teaspoon vanilla
½ cup chopped nuts

Combine white and brown sugars, cream, molasses and butter. Bring to a boil for 2 minutes. Add chocolate which has been grated and boil 5 minutes longer, stirring until well blended, and then only occasionally to prevent burning. Remove from heat and add vanilla. Stir until creamy. Pour into well-buttered pan and cut in squares.

❅ ❅ ❅ ❅ ❅ ❅

POTATO CANDY

1 medium-sized potato
1 pound icing sugar
1 cup coconut

1 teaspoon vanilla
1 square chocolate

Boil and mash the potato. Add icing sugar, coconut and vanilla. Mix well and press into a buttered pan. Melt the chocolate over hot water and pour over the top of the candy. Cut in squares.

DIVINITY FUDGE

2 cups white sugar
½ cup light corn syrup
¼ teaspoon salt

½ cup hot water
2 egg whites
1 teaspoon vanilla extract

Combine sugar, syrup, salt and hot water. Stir until dissolved and cook to the firm ball stage (248°). Remove from heat and combine stiffly beaten egg whites with the syrup, beating constantly until mixture holds its shape and loses its gloss. Add:

1 teaspoon vanilla
½ cup broken walnuts
Red and green cherries

Drop by dessertspoonfuls onto waxed paper, twirling into a peak; or pour into a buttered pan and cut in squares when cool.

✿ ✿ ✿ ✿ ✿ ✿

DELICIOUS PEPPERMINTS

2 cups white sugar
½ cup water
A few drops of essence of peppermint

Mix the sugar and water in a heavy saucepan and bring to the boil. Boil hard for about 3 minutes, then add the essence of peppermint. Remove from the stove and stir until white and creamy. Drop onto waxed paper, twirling the spoon as you do so or they will not be of a round shape. The dropping must be done quickly.

✿ ✿ ✿ ✿ ✿ ✿

SUGAR DATES AND WALNUT CREAMS

1 pound icing sugar
White of an egg
Flavoring to taste

Mix with a little cold water until a smooth pliable paste is formed. Have the dates stoned and put a little of the mixture inside the fruit. Dip filled dates in granulated sugar. Prepare in the same way for walnuts. Make the paste into flat neat circles; put half a walnut on each side and dip in granulated sugar.

194

CANDY APPLES

9 red apples   ¼ teaspoon salt
9 wooden skewers   ¼ teaspoon cream of tartar
3 cups white sugar   Red food coloring
1 cup water

Wash and polish apples. Remove stems and stick wooden skewers well down into stem end of apples. Combine sugar, cream of tartar, salt and water in a deep saucepan. Add red coloring until syrup is the desired color. Place saucepan over direct heat and stir until sugar is dissolved. Then cook rapidly without stirring to medium crack stage (290°). To prevent syrup turning into sugar do not stir while syrup is boiling. Remove from heat, keep warm and immediately begin dipping apples, one at a time. Twirl about and place, stick up, on waxed paper to cool and harden.

✿ ✿ ✿ ✿ ✿ ✿

The following "candy" was remembered by an elderly lady from the days of her childhood. She says she used to sneak into the kitchen to take little pieces from the glass jar in which it was stored and found especially good the little lumps of brown sugar that had not melted. Everyday her father would take a handful to work with him, to provide the sweet that finished off his lunch. She tells us her mother used it in different recipes or to top off bowls of cereal. We found it also makes a delicious topping for fruit desserts.

SCOTCH OATS

4 cups rolled oats   ⅔ cup melted butter
1 cup brown sugar (or maple
   sugar)

Spread the rolled oats on a flat shallow pan, together with the brown sugar which has been rubbed in with the fingers. Add the melted butter and stir to moisten. Put in a very hot oven for 10 minutes or a slower oven for 20-30 minutes. Store in glass jars.
Note: This will burn easily in a hot oven so must be stirred occasionally.

The number and variety of things that were candied and used as sweet-meats is rather astonishing. Many types of flowers, such as violets, marigolds, cowslips and primroses were candied and scattered on salads, desserts and iced cakes. If you are tempted to try this recipe for Candied Violets, do not use African violets.

CANDIED VIOLETS

1 cup sugar
¼ cup water

¼ teaspoon rosewater
(recipe follows)
OR ¼ teaspoon almond extract

Make a syrup of sugar and water and boil for awhile, stirring "if it gets uppity". Add rosewater or almond extract and let syrup cool. Now take the violets which you have gathered and put some of them, a few at a time, into the syrup. Let them stay there for a minute or so, being sure they are treated all over. Then remove to waxed paper with a skimmer or your fingers and put more in. If the syrup gets hard half-way through, cook up again adding a very little water. Leave the candied violets to dry thoroughly before storing. You may store them in glass jars if you are going to use them in a few weeks; otherwise, it is better to store all in a cardboard box in layers separated by waxed paper.

❀　❀　❀　❀　❀　❀

ROSEWATER

Boil ½ cup water and 1 quart of wild rose petals for 13 minutes, covered, and 5 minutes uncovered. Strain.

CURES AND TONICS

Almost every old cook book incorporated among its pages at least a few recipes for cures and preventatives. The larger printed books had an entire chapter devoted to the care of the sick. Such a reference guide was of extreme importance to our ancestors who, even in the direst emergencies, were often forced to face illness and death without the aid of a doctor.

The usual rule was "heal thyself" and this they attempted to do with remedies made from what was readily available. Many of these remedies were learned from the Micmacs who used the herbs and roots that grew in the forests that surrounded them.

Although superstitions played a major role in some of the cures, many of them were said to be very effective, and even some of our more immediate ancestors would scorn the doctor in preference to the home-made remedies that had been passed down through the generations.

Herbs were gathered in the evening before the dew came on them. These would then be dried, placed in separate paper bags, labelled and stored in the attic or in a special cupboard in the kitchen.

For treatment, herb teas were made by infusing the dried leaves or roots in boiling water. Sometimes, in the boiling process, it was deemed important to have some of the roots pointing up and others pointing down, and other little ceremonies ensured the potency of the medicine.

Peppermint or spearmint would be used to cure a cold; boils were treated with fir balsam or burdock roots; tansy was the remedy for blood poisoning; caraway was good for nursing mothers, cucumber juice for sunburn, and oak bark was boiled to a jelly to "cure" cancer. Pennyroyal, balm, wormwood, camomile, life-of-man, celandine, yarrow and marigold contained their properties and heal-all, and dandelion leaves were used every spring to cleanse the blood.

In almost every community there was a special person, usually a woman, who seemed to have a particular talent for healing. Often these women were called "Aunt" or "Granny", more as a title of respect than for any other reason. Believing that there was a plant designed by the Creator to cure each and every ailment, they had a remarkable knowledge of the medicinal properties of herbs and roots. With their little mortars and pestles they made their various concoctions and went around doing good to all who needed them.

Fevers and other disorders were thought to be caused by abnormal increases of water fluids (called humors) in the blood, so bleeding, blistering and purging were resorted to "for everything and anything".

In her history of Bridgetown, Nova Scotia, Elizabeth Ruggles Coward refers to a letter written by Mr. Andrew Henderson from Annapolis in 1832. A portion of that letter referred to medical treatment as follows:

> "For the last fifteen months I have not been able, till a Sunday or two ago, to take an active part in public worship. I feel you will hardly believe me when I tell you that the single article of molasses has saved my life.
>
> "In April of 1832 I was taken with a violent hemorrhage which continued with little cessation for three or four months. I had the medical assistance of Dr. Piper, Dr. Sinclair, Dr. Bayard of Annapolis, Dr. Lawson of the Garrison, Dr. Leslie, Dr. Bayard of Saint John and Dr. Dexter; from the force of the most powerful and poisonous medicines and numerous blisters between my shoulders the bleeding subsided, but I was left so diseased and feeble that no person

198

had the least hope of my life. A particular friend wrote to me to use a half pint of molasses daily, which he thought would help me. I did so and in a few days a visable alteration was incident in my person and feelings. I am now able to walk through the space of a mile and ride my horse at a full trot. I rode to Bridgetown, a distance of fifteen miles, without stopping."

The reference to molasses is most interesting since we know that quantities of that commodity were consumed in the old days. Bread and molasses was the usual snack for children, and every spring a mixture of sulphur and molasses was taken by one and all to cleanse the blood.

Rheumatism and lumbago were prevalent in the early days and many cures were devised for their treatment. Tuberculosis, or consumption as it was then called, took a heavy toll among the young adults, but the most dreaded of all diseases was diptheria, referred to as "the malignant destroyer of children".

The seaport of Halifax was particularly vulnerable to disease. From time to time, epidemics of smallpox carried off hundreds of people. In 1834, the Asiatic cholera took twenty or more lives each day for four months, and large trenches had to be dug for common graves. But the temperence societies claimed that the greatest killer of them all was strong drink. At a later time, one temperence member was to say: "Human life is longer now, since strong drinks and remedial measures for sickness are not in use as they were."

❋ ❋ ❋ ❋ ❋ ❋

An old prescription found by a fifth generation in the Densmore family in Noel, is recorded by Will R. Bird; Off Trail in Nova Scotia.

"Take one of the small powders every six hours and tomorrow evening put the plaster where I showed you. Be sparing on your diet and drink as little as possible. You can drink some of the tea of juniper berries 2 or 3 times a day. If you find a copping taste in your mouth or your gums become tender, you had better leave off for a day or two."

CURE FOR INFLUENZA

"This cure for stomach 'flu was learned from the Indians. Take about 2 cups of dry flour and tie in a cloth. Put in a pot of hot water and boil for 4 hours. When taken out this will be a hard ball. Cut the outside paste with a knife until you come to the dry flour. Grate the flour, which by now is too hard to break. When it is like powder cook it with milk and give to the patient. It is a sure cure. The old people used to call it pap."

✿ ✿ ✿ ✿ ✿ ✿

AN EXCELLENT REMEDY FOR A COLD

"Take a large teacupful of linseed, two pennyworth of stick licorice, and ¼ pound of sun raisins. Put these into 2 quarts of soft water, and let it simmer over a slow fire till it is reduced to one; then add to it ¼ pound brown sugar candy (pounded), a tablespoon of old rum, and a tablespoon of the best white-wine vinegar, or lemon juice. Drink half a pint at going to bed, and take a little when the cough is troublesome. This receipt generally cures the worst colds in 2 or 3 days, and if taken in time, may be said to be almost an infallible remedy. It is a most balsomic cordial for the lungs, without the opening qualities which endanger fresh colds on going out. It has been known to cure colds that have been almost settled into consumption, in less than three weeks. The rum and vinegar are best to be added only to the quantity you are going immediately to take; for if it is put into the whole it is apt to go flat."

REMEDY FOR DEBILITY

"One quart good old rye whiskey poured upon two pounds juicy beef-steak cut up small, cover it and let stand for twenty-four hours, then strain and bottle; dose from one tablespoonful to one wineglassful three times daily."

FOR RHEUMATISM

"One-half coffee cup best white wine vinegar, same quantity best turpentine, the well beaten whites of two eggs, mix together and put into a wide mouth bottle and shake thoroughly several times a day until well incorporated. Apply on a piece of red flannel, cover with oil silk. This is also an excellent remedy for bronchitis or any throat trouble that requires local application."

A GREAT RESTORATIVE - 1840

"Bake 2 calves' feet in 2 pints of water, and the same quantity of new milk; in a jar close-covered, 3½ hours. When cold remove the fat.

"Give a large teacupful the last and first thing. Whatever flavour is approved, give it by baking in it lemon-peel, cinnamon or mace. Add sugar after."

✿ ✿ ✿ ✿ ✿ ✿

ANOTHER RESTORATIVE

"Boil 1 ounce of isinglass-shavings, 40 Jamaica peppers (allspice), and a bit of brown crust of bread, in a quart of water to a pint, and strain it. This makes a pleasant jelly to keep in the house; of which a large spoonful may be taken in wine or water, milk, soup, or any way."

✿ ✿ ✿ ✿ ✿ ✿

FIG PASTE FOR CONSTIPATION

"One-half pound of good figs chopped fine, one-half pint of molasses, two ounces powdered senna leaves, one drachm fine powdered coriander seed; put the molasses on stove and let it come to a boil, then stir in all the rest and bring to a boil again. A teaspoonful once in awhile is a dose. It will keep, when covered, for a year."

201

GYPSEY WOMAN'S CURE

In an old Dartmouth cook book, the following recipe was written in a fine script, almost illegible with age.

"10c worth of linseed.   Boil like molasses.   ½ dozen lemons, Roast in oven.   5 cents worth white wine vinegar.   A little brandy.   10c worth rock sugar.   Mix all together.   Start with teaspoon in cup.   Take every day."

✿ ✿ ✿ ✿ ✿ ✿

GRANDMOTHER'S FAMILY SPRING BITTERS

"Mandrake root one ounce, dandelion root one ounce, burdock root one ounce, yellow dock root one ounce, prickly ash berries two ounces, marsh mallow one ounce, turkey rhubarb half an ounce, gentian one ounce, English camomile flowers one ounce, red clover tops two ounces.

"Wash the herbs and roots; put them into an earthen vessel, pour over two quarts of water that has been boiled and cooled; let it stand over night and soak; it must not boil, but be nearly ready to boil.   Strain it through a cloth, and add half a pint of good gin.   Keep it in a cool place.   Half a wine-glass taken as a dose twice a day.

"This is better than all the patent blood medicines that are in the market — a superior blood purifier, and will cure almost any malignant sore, by taking according to direction, and washing the sore with a strong tea of red raspberry leaves steeped, first washing the sore with castile soap, then drying with a soft cloth, and washing it with a strong tea of red raspberry leaves."

TUBERCULOSIS

"The Indian remedy for tuberculosis was a poultice of mustard put between pieces of flannel, which were then quilted. The flannel was worn between the shoulders because the lungs lie towards the back."

WET BED

"Eat pumpkin seeds for wet bed."

TO CURE A STING FROM BEE OR WASP

"Bind on common baking-soda, dampened with water. Or mix common earth with water to about the consistency of mud."

❋ ❋ ❋ ❋ ❋ ❋

The following is from an old newspaper clipping of around the turn of the century.

"In Friday evening's issue 'subscriber' asks for a remedy for RHEUMATISM. I would like her to try vegetable naptha, well massaging the affected parts with the above. It can be procured from any reliable chemist in as small a quantity as 10 cents worth. My mother has used this for acute rheumatism and found great relief.

"The following is an excellent remedy for CHILBLAINS: Melt one-half cup of lard and mix one good teaspoonful of mustard, then stand until cold. Use as any other ointment.

"For the benefit of mothers who may have children suffering with WHOOPING COUGH I recommend the following: Place a fresh egg (unbroken) in a covered jar, pour over the juice of lemons until covered (four should be sufficient) and let it stand about six days, when the egg-shell will be dissolved enough to beat up in the mixture. Then add 5 cents' worth of glycerine, 5 cents' worth of honey, and 5 cents' worth of paregoric, and shake up well before giving doses. It should be given in doses of one teaspoonful every four or five hours until the cough begins to die away.

"These have all been tried with good results."

INDEX

A

Acadian Dessert, An Old, 128

Acadienne Meat Pie, 59

Almond Paste, 146

Anadama Bread, 91

Apple Bread, 100

Apple Cake, Dried, 145

Apple Cider, 181

Apple Crisp, 131

Apple Dumplings, Baked, 127

Apple Jelly, 169

Apple Muffins, 110

Apple Pie, Sliced, 115

Apple Snow, 134

Apples, Baked, 130

Apples, Candy, 195

Atholl Brose, 188

Auld Man's Milk, 188

B

Backwoods Pie, 119

Baked Apple Dumplings, 127

Baked Apples, 130

Baked Beans, 81

Baked Finnan Haddie, 41

Baked Indian Pudding, 129

Baked Scallops, 44

Baked Shad, 42

Baked Spareribs with Sauerkraut, 59

Baked Stuffed Fish, 41

B - Con't

Bannock, 98

Barley Bread, 97

Barley Broth, Scotch, 27

Batter, Plain Fritter, 58

Beans, Baked, 81

Bean Hodge, 81

Bean Soup, Black, 27

Beans, Pickled, 175

Beaten Biscuits, 106

Beef, Pot Roast of, 51

Beef, Potted, 50

Beef, Spiced, 50

Beef Steak Pie, 52

Beef Stew with Dumplings, 51

Beef, To Corn a, 49

Beer, Ginger, 182

Beet Wine, Red, 185

Beets, Pickled, 175

Beverages, 177

Biscuits, Beaten, 106

Biscuits, Cream of Tartar, 107

Biscuits, Irish Potato, 108

Biscuits, Tea, 107

Black Bean Soup, 27

Blanc Mange, Irish Moss, 138

Blueberry Cake or Pudding, 148

Blueberry Griddle Cakes, 72

Blueberry Grunt, 129

B - Con't

Blueberry Muffins, 110

Blueberry Wine, 183

Boiled Dinner (Corned Beef), 49

Boiled Dinner (Fish), 37

Boiled Lobster, Fresh, 46

Boiled Salmon with Egg Sauce, 43

Boiled Tongue, 53

Boiling a Ham, Old Acadian Way of, 55

Brawn, English, 54

Bread, Anadama, 91

Bread, Apple, 100

Bread, Barley, 97

Bread, Carrot, 99

Bread Custard, 132

Bread, French, 92

Bread, Fried, 94

Bread, Irish Soda, 98

Bread, Nut, 100

Bread Pancakes, 71

Bread, Plum, 97

Bread, Rolled Oats, 91

Bread, Salt Rising, 92

Bread, Scottish Oat, 99

Bread, Spider Corn, 95

Bread, Spoon, 106

Bread, Steamed Brown, 93

Breads, 89

Breakfast Dish, Old Fashioned, 76

Breakfast Dishes, 69

B - Con't

Breakfast or Supper Dish, Lunenburg, 77
Brewis, 75
Brose, Atholl, 188
Broth, Scotch Barley, 27
Brown Bread, Steamed, 93
Brown Sauce, 148
Brown Sugar Sauce, 128
Buckwheat Pancakes, 71
Buckwheat Porridge, 74
Buns, Cinnamon, 104
Buns, Hot Cross, 105
Buns, Lazy, 105
Buns, Scones and Doughnuts, 101
Butter Tarts, 164
Buttermilk Pie, 119
Butterscotch Pie, 122
Butterscotch Sauce, 140
Butterscotch Toffee, 192

C

Cabbage, Creamed, 85
Cabbage Soup, 30
Cake, Blueberry, 148
Cake, Dark Fruit, 143
Cake, Delicious, 149
Cake, Dried Apple, 145
Cake, Farmer's Fruit, 145
Cake, French Cream, 153
Cake, Grandmother's Orange Raisin, 148
Cake, Happiness, 142
Cake, Irish Chocolate Potato, 153
Cake, Johnny, 109
Cake, Maple Johnny, 95
Cake, Maple Syrup, 150
Cake, Marble, 152
Cake, Minnehaha, 149
Cake, 1, 2, 3, 4, 151

C - Con't

Cake, Pork, 145
Cake, Pound, 150
Cake, Prince of Wales, 147
Cake, Simnel, 146
Cake, Sponge, 151
Cake, Sultana, 144
Cake, White Fruit, 144
Cakes, 141
Cakes, Eccles, 163
Cakes, Scotch, 161
Candied Violets, 196
Candies, 189
Candy Apples, 195
Candy, Molasses (La Tire) 192
Candy, Potato, 193
Candy, Vinegar, 191
Calf's Foot Jelly, How to Make, 138
Cape Breton Pork Pies, 164
Carrot Bread, 99
Carrot Marmalade, 171
Carrot Pudding, 125
Catchup, Tomato, 176
Catchup, Mushroom, 176
Cauliflower, Stuffed, 88
Champagne, Minute, 181
Champ, 87
Chappit Tatties, 87
Chicken Curry, 63
Chicken Fricot, 62
Chicken, Fried with Cream Gravy, 62
Chicken, Potted, 63
Chocolate Butter Icing, Rich, 154
Chocolate Potato Cake, Irish, 153
Chocolate Pie, 121
Chocolate Suace, 139
Chow Chow, 173
Chowder Bisque, Corn, 29
Chowder, Fish, 33

C - Con't

Chowder, Lobster, 34
Chowder, Nova Scotia Scallop, 33
Cider, Apple, 181
Cider, Mulled, 181
Cinnamon Buns, 104
Cinnamon Loaf, 94
Citrus Marmalade, 170
Clam Pie, 44
Clam Soup, 31
Clapshot, 88
Coarse Oatmeal Porridge, 74
Cobbler, Rhubarb, 131
Coconut Cream Pie, 121
Codfish Balls, 42
Codfish and Potatoes, 39
Colcannon, 84
Cookies and Little Cakes, 155
Cookies, Crispy Crunch, 160
Cookies, Jumbo Raisin, 162
Cookies, Maple Syrup, 158
Cookies, Old Fashioned Soft Molasses, 158
Cookies, Sugar, 157
Corn a Beef, To, 49
Corn Bread, Spider, 95
Corn Chowder Bisque, 29
Corn on the Cob, 88
Corn Relish, 172
Corned Beef and Cabbage, 49
Corned Beef Boiled Dinner, 49
Cornmeal Muffins, 109
Corn Meal Wine, 186
Cottage Cheese, 77
Cottage Pudding, 133
Crabapples, Spiced, 172
Cranberry Jelly, 170
Cream Gravy, 62

C - Con't

Cream of Potato Soup, 28

Cream of Tartar Biscuits, 107

Creamed Cabbage, 85

Creams, Walnut, 194

Crispy Crunch Cookies, 160

Cucumbers with Sour Cream, 85

Curd, Lemon, 171

Cure a Ham, To, 55

Cures and Tonics, 197

Curry, Chicken, 63

Custard, Bread, 132

Custard Sauce, 134

D

Dandelion Greens, 83

Dandelion Wine, 182

Dark Fruit Cake, 143

Dates, Sugar, 194

Delicious Cake, 149

Delicious Peppermints, 194

Dessert, Old Acadian, 128

Desserts, 123

Dike Mushrooms, 85

Divinity Fudge, 194

Doughboys, 51

Doughnuts, 111

Doughnuts, Scones and Buns, 101

Doughnuts, Sour Cream, 111

Doughnuts, Yeast or Raised, 112

Dried Apple Cake, 145

Drink for the Dog Days, 180

Duck, Mock, 52

Duck, Roast Wild, 65

Duff, Sailor's, 126

Dumplings, 51

Dumplings, Baked Apple, 127

D - Con't

Dumplings, Maple Syrup, 126

Dutch Mess, 39

E

Eccles Cakes, 163

Eel Soup, 31

Eels, Fried, 38

Eels, How to Skin, 31

Egg Sauce, 43

Eggs, Pickled, 176

Eggs, Scotch, 78

English Brawn, 54

English, The, 7

Everton Toffee, 192

F

Fanikaneekins, 94

Farmer's Fruit Cake, 145

Fiddleheads, 83

Finnan Haddie, Baked, 41

Fish, 35

Fish, Baked Stuffed, 41

Fish Chowder, 33

Flax-Breaking Party, 96

Fool, Gooseberry, 136

Forach, Scotch, 137

French Bread, 92

French Cream Cake, 153

French, The, 4

Fresh Boiled Lobster, 46

Fricassee, Rabbit, 68

Fricasseed Potatoes, 87

Fricot, Chicken, 62

Fried Bread, 94

Fried Chicken with Cream Gravy, 62

Fried Eels, 38

Fried Green Tomatoes, 86

Fried Salt Pork, 58

Fried Smelts, 38

Fritter Batter, 58

F - Con't

Frosting, Maple Sugar, 154

Fruit Cake, Dark, 143

Fruit Cake, Farmer's, 145

Fruit Cake, White, 144

Fruit Sauce Pickle, 175

Frumety, 75

Fudge, Divinity, 194

Fudge, Molasses, 193

G

Game Omelette, 68

Germans, The, 10

Ginger Beer, 182

Ginger Cream, 137

Ginger Snaps, 157

Gingerbread, 127

Goose, Roast, 65

Gooseberries, Spiced, 171

Gooseberry Fool, 136

Gooseberry Jam, 169

Grandmother's Orange Raisin Cake, 148

Grannie's Rocks, 162

Gravy, Cream, 62

Green Tomato Mincemeat 117

Green Tomatoes, Fried, 86

Greens, Dandelion, 83

Greens, Lamb's Quarters, 83

Greens, Sandfire, 82

Griddle Cakes, Blueberry, 72

Griddle Cakes, Old Fashioned, 72

Griddle Scones, 103

Grouse, To Roast, 66

Grunt, Blueberry, 129

Gypsy Pudding, 132

H

Haggis, 61

Half Hour Pudding, 133

H - Con't

Ham, Old Acadian Way of Boiling, 55
Ham, To Cure a, 55
Happiness Cake, 142
Hard Sauce, 140
Haymaker's Switchel, 187
Head Cheese, 58
Herring, Poached Kippered, 78
Herring, Potted, 40
Hodge, Bean, 81
Hodge Podge, 81
Hogmanay Shortbread, 161
Homemade Honey, 167
Homemade Pig's Pudding, 57
Homespun Pie, 116
Honey, Homemade, 167
Hot Cross Buns, 105
How to Make Calf's Foot Jelly, 138
How to Make Spruce Beer, 179
How to Skin Eels, 31

I

Ice Cream, Vanilla, 135
Icing, Maple Syrup, 154
Icing, Rich Chocolate Butter, 154
Indian Pudding, Baked, 129
Indians, The, 1
Irish Chocolate Potato Cake, 153
Irish Coffee, 188
Irish Moss Blanc Mange, 138
Irish Potato Biscuits, 108
Irish Potato Cakes, 73
Irish Soda Bread, 98
Irish Stew, 54
Irish, The, 16

J

Jam, Gooseberry, 169
Jam, Pumpkin, 168
Jam, Rhubarb and Pineapple, 168
Jam, Rose Hip, 167
Jam, Strawberry, 168
Jams and Pickles, 165
Jelly, Apple, 169
Jelly, Cranberry, 170
Jelly Roll, Old Fashioned, 152
Johnny Cake, 109
Johnny Cake, Maple, 95
Jumbo Raisin Cookies, 162

K

Kartoffelsuppe, 30
Kedgeree, 37
Kippered Herring, Poached, 78
Kisses, Velvet, 191
Kohl Cannon, 84
Kohl Slaw, 84

L

La Tire (Saint Catherine), 192
Lamb's Quarters, 83
Lazy Buns, 105
Lemonade, 187
Lemon Curd, 171
Lemon Meringue Pie, 122
Lemon Sauce, 139
Levi's Pie, 131
Little Cakes and Cookies, 155
Liver Loaf, Pork, 59
Lobster Chowder, 34
Lobster, Fresh Boiled, 46
Lobster Soup, 34
Lobster Stew, 34
Lobsters, Old Style, 46

L - Con't

Long Johns, 158
Lunenburg Sausage, 57

M

Mackerel, Soused, 40
Maids of Honor, 163
Mangle Wine, 184
Maple Johnny Cake, 95
Maple Mousse, 136
Maple Sugar Frosting, 154
Maple Sugar Pie, 118
Maple Syrup Cake, 150
Maple Syrup Cookies, 158
Maple Syrup Dumplings, 126
Maple Syrup Icing, 154
Maple Syrup Pie, 118
Marble Cake, 152
Marmalade, Carrot, 171
Marmalade, Citrus, 170
Meats, 47
Meat Pie a L'Acadienne, 59
Mincemeat, Green Tomato, 117
Mincemeat, Old Fashioned, 116
Minnehaha Cake, 149
Minute Champagne, 181
Mock Duck, 52
Molasses Candy (La Tire), 192
Molasses Cookies, Soft, 158
Molasses Fudge, 193
Molasses Pie, 117
Molasses Taffy, 191
Mousse, Maple, 136
Muffins, Apple, 110
Muffins, Blueberry, 110
Muffins, Cornmeal, 109
Muffins, Oatmeal, 109
Mulled Cider, 181

M - Con't

Mushroom Catchup, 176
Mushrooms, Dike, 85
Mussel Stew, 32
Mustard Pickles, Sweet, 174

N

Negroes, The, 22
Negus, Soda, 180
Never-Fail Pie Crust, 115
New Englanders, The, 13
Nova Scotia Scallop
  Chowder, 33
Nut Bread, 100

O

Oat Bread, Scottish, 99
Oat Cakes, 160
Oatcakes, Pictou County,
  159
Oatmeal Muffins, 109
Oatmeal Porridge, 74
Oats, Scotch, 195
Old Acadian Way of Boiling
  a Ham, 55
Old Fashioned Breakfast
  Dish, 76
Old Fashioned Buckwheat
  Pancakes, 71
Old Fashioned Griddle
  Cakes, 72
Old Fashioned Jelly Roll,
  152
Old Fashioned Lunenburg
  Breakfast or Supper Dish,
  77
Old Fashioned Mincemeat,
  116
Old Fashioned Plum Loaf,
  97
Old Style Nova Scotia
  Lobsters, 46
Omelette, Game, 68
One, Two, Three, Four
  Cake, 151

O - Con't

Orange Pudding, 130
Orange Raisin Cake,
  Grandmother's, 148
Orange Sauce, 140
Oyster Stew, 32
Oysters on the Half Shell, 45
Oysters, Scalloped, 45

P

Pancakes, Bread, 71
Pancakes, Old Fashioned,
  Buckwheat, 71
Parsley Wine, 185
Parsnip Wine, 184
Partridge, To Roast, 66
Partridge with Cabbage, 66
Pate a La Rapure, 64
Pea Soup, Split, 28
Peppermints, Delicious, 194
Pheasant, To Roast, 66
Pickle, Fruit Sauce, 175
Pickled Beans, 175
Pickled Beets, 175
Pickled Eggs, 176
Pickles and Jams, 165
Pickles, Sweet Mustard, 174
Pickles, Ten Day, 174
Pictou County Oatcakes,
  159
Pie, Apple, 115
Pie, Backwoods, 119
Pie, Beef Steak, 52
Pie, Buttermilk, 119
Pie, Butterscotch, 122
Pie, Chocolate, 121
Pie, Clam, 44
Pie, Coconut Cream, 121
Pie Crust, Never-Fail, 115
Pie, Homespun, 116
Pie, Lemon Meringue, 122
Pie, Maple Sugar, 118

P - Con't

Pie, Maple Syrup, 118
Pie, Meat A L'Acadienne,
  59
Pie, Molasses, 117
Pie, Raisin Cream, 120
Pie, Rappie, 64
Pie, Sliced Apple, 115
Pie, Vinegar, 120
Pies, 113
Pig's Pudding, 57
Pikelets, 73
Pineapple and Rhubarb
  Jam, 168
Plain White Rolls, 104
Planked Salmon, 43
Plum Loaf, Old Fashioned,
  97
Plum Pudding, 125
Poached Kippered Herring,
  78
Popovers, 108
Pork Cake, 145
Pork, Fried Salt, 58
Pork Liver Loaf, 59
Pork Pie Tourtieres, 56
Pork Pies, Cape Breton, 164
Pork, Salt with Creamy
  Gravy, 78
Porridge Bread, 91
Porridge, Buckwheat, 74
Porridge, Coarse Oatmeal,
  74
Port Wine, 183
Posset, To Make a Sack,
  180
Pot Roast of Beef, 51
Pot Roast, Venison, 67
Potato Biscuits, Irish, 108
Potato Cake, Irish
  Chocolate, 153
Potato Cakes, Irish, 73
Potato Candy, 193
Potato Soup, Cream of, 28

P - Con't

Potato Stuffing, 65

Potatoes and Salt Herring, 39

Potatoes, Fricasseed, 87

Potatoes, Scotch Stoved, 87

Potted Beef, 50

Potted Chicken, 63

Potted Herring, 40

Pound Cake, 150

Poutine a Trou, 128

Poutines Rapees, 56

Prince of Wales Cake, 147

Pudding, Baked Indian, 129

Pudding, Blueberry, 148

Pudding, Carrot, 125

Pudding, Cottage, 133

Pudding, Gypsy, 132

Pudding, Half Hour, 133

Pudding, Orange, 130

Pudding, Plum, 125

Pudding, Snow, 134

Pudding, Stir, 77

Puddings, Queen of, 132

Pumpkin Jam, 168

Pumpkin Soup, 29

Q

Quail, To Roast, 66

Queen of Puddings, 132

R

Rabbit Fricassee, 68

Rabbit Stew with Dumplings, 67

Raised Doughnuts, 112

Raisin Cookies, Jumbo, 162

Raisin Cream Pie, 120

Rappie Pie, 64

Raspberry Vinegar, 187

Red Beet Wine, 185

Red Pepper Relish, Sweet, 173

R - Con't

Relish, Corn, 172

Relish, Rhubarb, 172

Relish, Sweet Red Pepper, 173

Rhubarb Cobbler, 131

Rhubarb and Pineapple Jam, 168

Rhubarb Relish, 172

Rhubarb Wine, 186

Rich Chocolate Butter Icing, 154

Roast Goose, 65

Roast Wild Duck, 65

Rocks, Grannie's, 162

Rolled Oats Bread, 91

Rolls, Plain White, 104

Rose Hip Jam, 167

Rosewater, 196

S

Sack Posset, To Make a, 180

Sailor's Duff, 126

Sally Lunns, 93

Salmon, Boiled with Egg Sauce, 43

Salmon, Planked, 43

Salt Herring and Potatoes, 39

Salt Pork, Fried, 58

Salt Pork with Creamy Gravy, 78

Salt Rising Bread, 92

Sandfire Greens, 82

Sausage Meat, 58

Sauce, Brown, 148

Sauce, Brown Sugar, 128

Sauce, Butterscotch, 140

Sauce, Chocolate, 139

Sauce, Custard, 134

Sauce, Egg, 43

Sauce, Hard, 140

Sauce, Lemon, 139

S - Con't

Sauce, Molasses, 140

Sauce, Orange, 140

Sauce, White, 43

Scallop Chowder, Nova Scotia, 33

Scalloped Oysters, 45

Scallops, Baked, 44

Scallops Baked in their Shells, 44

Scones, Buns and Doughnuts, 101

Scones, Griddle, 103

Scones, Sultana, 103

Scouse, 76

Scotch Barley Broth, 27

Scotch Cakes, 161

Scotch Cheese, 76

Scotch Eggs, 78

Scotch Forach, 137

Scotch Oats, 195

Scotch Stoved Potatoes, 87

Scots, The, 19

Scottish Oat Bread, 99

Seed Wheat Wine, 186

Shad, Baked, 42

Shortbread, Hogmanay, 161

Shortcake, Strawberry, 130

Simnel Cake, 146

Skirl in the Pan, 75

Slaw, Kohl, 84

Slow Pokes, 40

Sliced Apple Pie, 115

Smelts, Fried, 38

Snaps, Ginger, 157

Snow Pudding, 134

Soda Bread, Irish, 98

Soda Negus, 180

Solid Syllabub, 135

Solomon Gundy, 40

Soup, Black Bean, 27

Soup, Clam, 31

210

S - Con't

Soup, Cream of Potato, 28
Soup, Eel, 31
Soup, Lobster, 34
Soup, Pumpkin, 29
Soup, Split Pea, 28
Soupe au Chou, 30
Soups and Chowders, 25
Sour Cream Doughnuts, 111
Soused Mackerel, 40
South Shore Boiled Dinner, 37
Spareribs with Sauerkraut, Baked, 59
Spiced Beef, 50
Spiced Crabapples, 172
Spiced Gooseberries, 171
Spider Corn Bread, 95
Split Pea Soup, 28
Sponge Cake, 151
Spoon Bread, 106
Spruce Beer, 179
Spruce Beer, How to Make, 179
Steamed Brown Bread, 93
Stew, Beef with Dumplings, 51
Stew, Irish, 54
Stew, Lobster, 34
Stew, Mussel, 32
Stew, Oyster, 32
Stew, Rabbit, 67
Stir Pudding, 77
Stovies, 87
Strawberry Jam, 168
Strawberry Shortcake, 130
Stuffed Cauliflower, 88
Stuffed Tomatoes, 86
Stuffing, Potato, 65

S - Con't

Succotash, Summer, 82
Succotash, Winter, 82
Sucre La Creme, 193
Sugar Cookies, 157
Sugar Dates, 194
Sugar Makin' Time, 118
Sultana Cake, 144
Sultana Scones, 103
Summer Succotash, 82
Supper Dish, Old Fashioned Lunenburg, 77
Supper Dishes, 69
Sweet Mustard Pickles, 174
Sweet Red Pepper Relish 173
Sweetbreads, 60
Switchel, Haymaker's, 187
Syllabub, Solid, 135

T

Taffy, Molasses, 191
Tarts, Butter, 164
Tatties 'n Herrin', 39
Tatties 'n Neeps, 88
Tea Biscuits, 107
Ten Day Pickles, 174
To Corn a Beef, 49
To Cure a Ham, 55
To Make a Sack Posset, 180
To Roast Partridge, Pheasant, Quail or Grouse, 66
Toffee, Butterscotch, 192
Tomato Catchup, 176
Tomato Mincemeat, Green, 117
Tomatoes, Fried Green, 86
Tomatoes, Stuffed, 86

T - Con't

Tongue, Boiled, 53
Tongues and Sounds, 38
Tourtieres, Pork Pie, 56
Tripe, 60
Turtles in Shells, 60

V

Vanilla Ice Cream, 135
Veal Roll, 53
Vegetables, 79
Velvet Kisses, 191
Venison Pot Roast, 67
Vinegar Candy, 191
Vinegar Pie, 120
Vinegar, Raspberry, 187
Violets, Candied, 196

W

Walnut Creams, 194
White Fruit Cake, 144
White Rolls, Plain, 104
White Sauce, 43
Wild Duck, Roast, 65
Wine, Blueberry, 183
Wine Corn Meal, 186
Wine, Dandelion, 182
Wine, Mangle, 184
Wine, Parsley, 185
Wine, Parsnip, 184
Wine, Port, 183
Wine, Red Beet, 185
Wine, Rhubarb, 186
Wine, Seed Wheat, 186
Winter Succotash, 82

Y

Yeast Doughnuts, 112